D1260133

The Power of Forgiveness

The
Power
of
Forgiveness

Eva Mozes Kor

CRP
CENTRAL RECOVERY PRESS
LAS VEGAS

Central Recovery Press (CRP) is committed to publishing exceptional materials addressing addiction treatment, recovery, and behavioral healthcare topics.

For more information, visit www.centralrecoverypress.com.

Publisher: Central Recovery Press
            3321 N. Buffalo Drive
            Las Vegas, NV 89129

26 25 24 23 22 21   1 2 3 4 5

ISBN: 978-1-949481-44-0 (paper)
       978-1-949481-45-7 (e-book)

Library of Congress Control Number: 2020947989

Photo of Eva Mozes Kor used courtesy of CANDLES Holocaust Museum and Education Center.

Publisher's Note
This book contains general information about trauma, surviving abuse, and healing. The information contained herein is not medical advice. This book is not an alternative to medical advice from your doctor or other professional healthcare provider.

Our books represent the experiences and opinions of their authors only. Every effort has been made to ensure that events, institutions, and statistics presented in our books as facts are accurate and up-to-date. To protect their privacy, the names of some of the people, places, and institutions in this book may have been changed.

Cover design and interior by Sara Streifel, Think Creative Design.

Contents

Foreword

"It's as simple as making a decision."

During the many conversations I had with Eva on the topic of forgiveness, she made it sound so easy. Eva's idea was that forgiveness is a simple decision with huge consequences—both positive and negative. Through forgiveness, she felt free from the anger and hurt. She felt fortunate to discover the power of forgiveness and wanted to make it available to other people. She was firm in her belief that forgiveness would heal victims, and she wanted to shout it from the mountaintops. She shared her message whenever and wherever she could. In spite of this, she was criticized for forgiving what some feel is unforgiveable, the murder of her family. Still, she believed in her cure for victimhood.

It was my privilege to spend a lot of time with Eva before her death, both personally and professionally. We traveled together locally for doctors visits and nationally to lectures and interviews. Sitting in waiting rooms or cars, we would discuss our calendars, new projects she was creating for the staff, or her train ride from the ghetto to Auschwitz. It did not matter the purpose; Eva was always working, always thinking. That is one of the things I loved most about her: she continued to find new ways to do things, to help people.

Even before these conversations with Eva, I believed in forgiveness, or at least in the idea of letting go of anger and hate. It is just too heavy and difficult to carry for extended periods of time. Like many, my husband feels the opposite and believes revenge is warranted for wrongful acts. One of the powers of Eva's forgiveness was that she brought the idea to light and allowed people to have the conversation. While she wanted them to forgive, the debate of the idea was another important part of her legacy.

You can learn more about Eva's story at the museum she founded, CANDLES Holocaust Museum and Education Center, located in Terre Haute, Indiana. Eva loved acronyms; CANDLES stands for Children of Auschwitz Nazi Deadly Lab Experiments Survivors. The mission is to spread hope, healing, respect, and responsibility, while shining a light on the Holocaust.

The terrible things that Eva endured give strength and real power to her forgiveness. If she could forgive, I feel strongly that anyone can. Forgiveness is Eva's gift to the world. I hope you'll consider it as a way to heal from any pain that you have endured. Together, we can heal the world through forgiveness, one person at a time.

Leah Hemeyer Simpson
MA Holocaust and Genocide Studies
Executive Director of CANDLES Holocaust Museum
and Education Center

Prologue

I know hate. I know only too well how it feels, in all of its variations. How it spreads through one's stomach—the hate—and how it increasingly steers your thoughts. And I know what it's like to long for revenge.

What would happen?

Today, I can still see myself traveling through Upper Bavaria, to visit a man who worked as a camp doctor in Auschwitz, where I lost my family and my childhood. He was a colleague of Dr. Mengele's, the man who humiliated and abused me, who forced me to look death in the eyes.

Have I already mentioned that I know how hate feels? Oh, do I!

So I am driven through Roßhaupten, a picturesque village in Allgäu, surrounded by meadows and mountains, with a baroque church with an onion tower around which the village spreads to the edge of an alpine lake. Around two thousand people live there. And I still remember my unease. My anger (fury?) at the world and at the Germans, in particular. The word *forgiveness* didn't exist in my vocabulary. It wasn't even remotely in my mind. Even the idea of actually meeting a Nazi from Auschwitz was crazy.

I became more and more nervous with each kilometer.

⁜ ⁜ ⁜

Beforehand, I had seen all kinds of documentaries, anything I could get my hands on, and this man, Dr. Hans Münch, was a typical Nazi. Tall, stately, as one would say. Even as an eighty-two-year-old. He looked a little like Laurence Olivier in *The Marathon Man*. I was afraid of him.

But there was no turning back now. Despite my sleeplessness, my scruples, despite all my reservations that the whole trip would end in tears. I had to find out about the viruses or bacteria that my sister and I had been injected with. Miriam had just died the previous year because the doctors had been defeated by her uncommon side effects. So I had to meet this former Nazi doctor.

Because I have a rule: if I agree to do something, then I follow through with it. I honor my word.

I also wanted to find out what went through this man's mind. How could he have worked in the camp; how could he live with the atrocities? How could he continue *living* after Auschwitz?

A nice house, I remember. Surrounded by a well-tended garden. And Dr. Münch opened the front door with a friendly smile. And shook my hand.

I wasn't expecting that. In my mind, this man was an arrogant Nazi, who was oh so generously granting me, a poor survivor, an audience—but he wasn't that way. In my mind, Germans were serious, no one would smile. I expected to see a monster: SS-Untersturmführer Hans Münch, camp doctor in Auschwitz, Hitler's henchman in humanity's worst crime.

But he is *nice*. A polite old gentleman with a white beard.

At the same time, a frenetic TV team is circling us. They want to document my visit, and there are several camera operators and sound technicians, which creates a bizarre backdrop to this intimate moment. A Dutch producer who continually worries that if I ask something critical, Dr. Münch will suddenly break off the meeting. A cameraman complains about the poor lighting.

At the same time, the Nazi doctor continues to bring me cushions. Multiple times. And all of that doesn't add up with my plan. The previous night had been a sleepless one. I lose control.

"Why are you bringing me so many pillows?" I ask.

"I want to make sure that you are comfortable," Dr. Münch answers. A Nazi who cares about me sitting comfortably, it makes no sense to me. I am afraid about suddenly losing my voice when I start the interview. I am so incredibly unprepared.

⋆ ⋆ ⋆

So I begin by asking stupid questions. A little small talk—with a doctor from Auschwitz, who saw thousands of people die! But there is no alternative, first because this producer insists on prophesying a sudden stop to the interview and because I decided to start with innocuous questions and then only ask the important questions at the end. Like: What do you know about the experiments in Auschwitz? What did you do after the end of the war?

"What are your hobbies?" I ask as a start.

What do I care about the hobbies of a Nazi criminal? But I want to get a feel for his mentality, tease out what makes him tick. Face-to-face.

"I like to read," Dr. Münch responds, "and I hunt for mushrooms." He answers in a very friendly tone, he listens to me. Which I don't understand. I'm missing the fiendish aspect.

"What was your life like in Auschwitz?"

My mouth is dry.

"The reality in Auschwitz was," he responded quietly, "that the entire guard personnel were drunk in the evening. The only person sitting next to me who wasn't completely drunk was Mengele. So he was the only person I could talk to. But he told me nothing about the experiments. Those were top secret."

Dr. Münch said that my sister Miriam and I would have been killed sooner or later. Mengele's experiments had saved us from being killed for a while. Mengele had told him in Auschwitz that the twins should be thankful to him for that.

"You were in Auschwitz, Dr. Münch—did you know where the gas chambers were? Did you look inside them? Do you know anything about them?"

I can't wait any longer!

Dr. Münch swallowed and lowered his head. Then he looked up, but his eyes, which had looked at me in such a friendly and gentle way, suddenly looked through me, staring into nowhere. He rasped more than he spoke, "That is my problem . . ." He swallowed again. "That is the nightmare that I have to live with daily. . . ."

For nearly fifty years.

Then he added, "All of my memories of Auschwitz made it so I had no more joy in life." Before he withdrew with shame and horror into himself.

In front of me is a broken man. I am silent.

1

Auschwitz

There had been *rumors*.

But we lived at the end of the world.

We were the only Jewish family in Portz, a tiny village of 100 inhabitants in Siebenbürgen, in the middle of Romania. In Transylvania. My mother's and father's families had lived in Romania for generations, and they always tried to maintain friendly contact. We couldn't have risked conflict; we were Jews.

Moreover, the *rumors* concerned Germany.

✶ ✶ ✶

I had two older sisters. In all of our family photos you can see how Miriam and I, and our older sisters, Edit and Aliz, wore identical clothes in our respective pairs.

Life was very simple for us, living in this rural seclusion. Miriam and I got up early in the morning, at least in summer, even before our parents, and watered the plants in the garden.

Then we all ate breakfast together. Afterward it was time to tend to the chickens and ducks and clean the house. My father took care of the cows. We had no idea about what was going on in the rest of the world. But we would find out very soon.

In 1940, the National Socialist German Reich forced Romania to hand over a section of Siebenbürgen to Hungary. It was a crescent-shaped section along the north and northeast border. Our village was a part of this agreement, although only Romanians lived there.

At this time my father and Uncle Aaron went to Palestine for several months and then returned to Portz. Upon their return, Uncle Aaron and his wife sold all their land, livestock, and possessions and prepared to emigrate. My father urged my mother to follow Uncle Aaron, to cash in everything and emigrate to Palestine with the family.

But my mother refused. For her, that was all too hasty, not properly thought through.

"No," she said. "With four small children, I cannot move away."

This place was not just any old address to my mother; it was her home. She loved her flower beds in the front yard and her vegetable garden out back, she loved her cows, all the chickens and geese. But what was hardest for her was the thought of leaving her sick mother behind.

"We have to leave before the conditions get worse for us here," my father urged. He was worried by the news he was hearing about the increasing persecution of Jews throughout the whole country and in Europe.

"Palestine?" my mother answered. "How will we get along in Palestine? I don't want to live in the desert."

She wanted to believe that the rumors circulating of Jews being persecuted by the Germans and their head of state, Adolf Hitler, were no more than that—rumors. Although the harassment of the villagers and their children was becoming increasingly threatening and more frequent.

But somehow no one could imagine that Hitler and his henchmen could be interested in Romania. Neither could my father. "The Nazis would never come to a little village like ours," he said in the end. That was the end of the discussion.

$$\star \ \star \ \star$$

Sure enough, Hitler never came. But the Hungarian police did. When they pulled us from our home in 1944, all of the residents of Portz were standing in the road. It was the only road leading through the village. And all of our neighbors stood there to watch. No one said a word. I don't know what was going through their minds. They were familiar people who came from their farmhouses and lined up along the edge of the road. And there were kids from our school—they all gawked at us. No one tried to stop the police from taking us away. No one said a word.

Even my best friend was standing with the group. I looked at her as we were pushed past. She looked at the ground.

They pushed us into a horse-drawn wagon. There were no written documents or court orders; we were simply taken away. About a five hours' drive away, where we were forced to move into a ghetto there, together with more than 7,000 other Jews from the surrounding area. Miriam and I had never seen so many people before. We learned that moreover, all the Jews living in Nazi-occupied areas were to be relocated to towns specifically allocated to them. And it wasn't the Germans who were holding us prisoner in this ghetto; it was the Hungarians.

It was also the Hungarians who whipped my father until his entire back was bleeding. And it was the Hungarians who burned his fingernails and toenails with candles. Because they were convinced that my parents had hidden valuables in the farm— valuables they wanted to acquire for themselves. It was terrible.

Miriam and I felt helpless. We were nine years old. Children! And we expected our parents to protect us. But they could do nothing, nothing at all. Mother and Father were prisoners, just like we were.

And we children couldn't even comfort our father.

⋆ ⋆ ⋆

One morning in May 1944, after five long weeks in the ghetto, we were instructed to leave our last belongings behind. To undertake a new *journey*.

A last resettlement.

Miriam and I put on our identical wine-red dresses and boarded a cattle car.

Of course it wasn't a journey, but yet another nightmare lasting several days. Around 100 people were cooped up in the tiny train car without seats, without food or drink, and the only light came from a little window in the ceiling. No fresh air. There was a bucket in the corner, around which pieces of paper were scattered, which led me to believe that it was supposed to be the toilet. But since there was nothing to eat or drink, I didn't feel the urge to go. It was late May, and inside it was scorching hot. The wood and metal of the train car got hotter and hotter.

The car was filled with the sounds of adults trying to suppress their tears and the sounds of children who had caught the obvious desperation in the air. We didn't know where we were being taken. The train was hurtling at top speed. We were afraid they would take us to a Hungarian work camp, like the Hungarian soldiers who picked us up had predicted. If there were any stops at all, it was only to refuel. Or to load something. Although I didn't know what. In any case something mechanical since it was clear that they never would have stopped for the people in the cattle car, for us, that is. So it must have been for the train, for the engines.

We tried to talk with the guards when the train stopped. Each train car was separated by a cubby where a guard stood with a machine gun. We asked him for water. We were incredibly thirsty. Their response was always the same: "Five gold watches." The adults collected everything they could find and passed it through the window hole, which was covered with barbed wire. Then the guard would reach for a bucket of water outside and poured some through the ceiling window. I stretched my head upward, held out my tongue, opened my mouth as wide as I could, but I didn't get any water. Just a few drops at most.

At each stop, the same grim ritual was repeated. And a thought raced through my head, *Why do we always ask for water, why do we always collect gold watches when the result is the same each time? That is, no water.*

But I wouldn't have had the courage to ask my parents about it. Today I understand that people who fear for their lives cannot think straight. They retreat completely into themselves. Today I understand why we did that. When I look back, it's still a mystery to me how we managed to even survive the journey. People died in other train cars, frequently, even. I have a vague memory that a person collapsed in our car, but I am not 100 percent certain.

✶ ✶ ✶

All of a sudden, we had reached our destination.

But nothing happened. For one or two hours, we heard countless German voices screaming orders. The doors of the train still remained shut.

I was just ten years old; I was a little girl, but I had a pretty clear idea about what would happen next. We had crossed over into German-occupied territory, German voices were everywhere, German guards—so we would be murdered next. At that time in the Hungarian ghetto, there had already been rumors that the Jews were taken to Germany to be murdered there. We didn't know where, we didn't know how. But our last hope had always been: Don't get taken to Germany.

That hope had now evaporated. In the cattle car, screams and prayers sounded everywhere, and the desperate pleas for water were no longer answered.

Father took us aside. "Promise me that if any of you survives this terrible war, you will go to Palestine, where your Uncle Aaron lives and where we Jews can live in peace." We four sisters readily agreed to do so.

✶ ✶ ✶

Outside, countless cries and orders rang out. A constant stream of German orders. Dogs were barking at us from all directions.

Then the doors of the cattle car opened, squeaking, and the SS men ordered us to come out. The people got up with an effort, sometimes tangled together, cowering. The guards grabbed other people and pulled them to the right or left on the selection ramp. The people from the cattle car began to cry, to call out and scream, all at the same time. Each person was looking for family members, who had all been separated. Men were separated from women, children from parents. The whole scene was punctuated by orders. "Fast!" I cannot remember even one of these guards speaking in a friendly or gentle manner, even once. *"Raus!"* ("Out!").

We helped the older people out of the car ourselves. Some mothers held their children close, while other children were already wandering around outside, thankful for the fresh air after the long confinement.

"Schnell! Schnell!" ("Quickly, quickly!")

I still hear these German words today. Their sound still rings in my ears. The aggression.

I can still see the whole scene before me; everything seemed so incredibly lifeless, bleak, and hopeless. High barbed wire fences, barbed wire period, everywhere, in front of windows and doors. Concrete watchtowers everywhere. Dark buildings, like a dark premonition. Soldiers leaned out of the buildings and pointed their guns at us. Guard dogs, who were kept on a lead by other SS soldiers, reared on their leashes, barking and snarling. It was a terrible place, stark, lonely. The sky was overcast and gray. My first thought was, *I don't know if there is a hell, but if there were, it would look like this.*

✴ ✴ ✴

Up until then, as we would later find out, the groups who were selected for the gas chambers would walk the three-kilometer walk from Auschwitz to Birkenau. However, in 1944, a direct railway connection to Birkenau had been built. And it practically stopped right at the doors of the crematorium, known as KII and KIII.

And this is where we stood.

"Out!"

This place was confusing and loud. There was a terrible smell in the air. It reminded me of burned chicken feathers.

The ramp was perhaps eighty-five feet long, thirty-five feet wide (approx. 26 m x 11 m). I don't think there is any other piece of land on this planet like this that has witnessed millions of people being ripped away from their families, just like that.

Where people shriek. Where people scream. Where there is so much desperation.

My mother took Miriam and me by the hand. Her youngest children. In all of the confusion and chaos. She probably thought that as long as she held both of us by the hand, she could protect us.

All around us, the ceaseless barking of the dogs.

The orders.

The cries, the cries, the cries . . . I still hear it all today. Particularly the children crying for their parents. The parents crying for their babies.

While everything else happened so fast.

The SS guards moved purposefully between the groups of people, as if they were searching for something. I looked around and felt Miriam's shivering body next to mine. But where was my father?

An SS man ran toward us. He called out in German, "Twins! Twins!"

He had this impression since Miriam and I were dressed alike, both in red dresses, and because we looked similar.

"Are they twins?" he asked my mother.

She hesitated. "Is that good?"

"Yes," answered the guard.

"They are twins," my mother replied.

Without a word of explanation, the man tore us from her hand and pulled us aside.

I had lost sight of my older siblings, Edit and Aliz, and my father right after we had gotten off the cattle car. We screamed and cried as they dragged us away. But the German guard paid no attention to our pleas. All of that took maybe ten minutes, not more.

Ten minutes . . . and I never saw any of them again.

⚹ ⚹ ⚹

We were crying. My mother was crying.

She disappeared into the crowd. I can still remember how she desperately stretched out her arms out as they dragged her away. Naked desperation was written on her face. I couldn't even say goodbye (*tschö*) to her. But as it was, I couldn't grasp that this was really the last moment I would ever see my mother.

Never . . .

The guards separated people into groups on the selection ramp. Young men and women. Children and older people.

Because of our identical wine-red dresses and because we were easy to spot as identical twins in the crowd of dirty, exhausted Jewish prisoners, they picked us out. Later, I often wondered why the guards didn't notice my two older sisters. They were wearing identical white sailor's dresses with blue collars. My mother always sewed everything in pairs, always in the same design. Maybe Edit and Aliz let the truth slip out in their naiveté. Namely that they weren't twins. The Nazis killed them. Edit was fourteen years old; Aliz was twelve.

In the meantime, maybe a half hour had passed. Considering how many people had been on the trains, it's still unimaginable for me how it all happened so fast.

We were only ten years old, but from then on, Miriam and I had no more family. We were alone, without any idea of what that meant. And all for one reason—because we were born Jews. And I didn't understand what was so wrong with that.

Miriam and I held on to each other while we were brought to a group of twelve pairs of twins. Soon we would stand before Josef Mengele, the Nazi doctor who had been known as the "Angel of Death" since 1943. He was the one who determined who would live or die on the ramp. Because he wanted to create a new race. I don't know whether all of these twins were on our train or whether the guards had discovered them over the course of the general selection.

We were a group of twenty-six children, all afraid and confused. We were constantly looking around for other people. Surrounded by SS men with guns who were giving us orders. They watched us like a group of dangerous criminals. Children! On the way to our barracks.

I remember a group of people standing close to the barrack. They were skin and bones, accompanied by other SS guards with huge dogs. Returning from some kind of work. Pale and starving, and I still remember thinking, they look like walking skeletons.

One poor soul from our group stepped forward and said in German, "Little child, little child . . ." In turn, one of the guards let two powerful German shepherds off their leashes who were barking with deep, throaty voices. "Attack!" was the command. And the dogs obeyed. They ran toward the troublemaker and bit into her again and again. They literally tore her apart before our eyes.

We were supposed to get undressed in another dark building.

Would it happen now? I had been separated from my parents and my siblings and had heard terrible things. I was prepared for anything. I didn't feel anything anymore; I was physically and mentally numb. Like a nightmare—but a nightmare would end as soon as I opened my eyes. My beloved mother would surely wake me and hug me soon . . .

But I didn't wake up.

★ ★ ★

Today, I think that the sudden, brutal separation from my mother put me in shock. In this frozen state, naked in a group of strangers, clueless about what would happen next, waiting felt like an eternity.

And all of our hair was cut short.

Then we showered. Our clothing was disinfected with a lice-killing chemical. Wearing our own clothes was a so-called "privilege" for us twins, which the other prisoners didn't have.

But our clothes had large red crosses on the back. They were similar to the yellow star in the ghettos and were used to identify us so we couldn't run away.

The new arrivals received tattoos on their arms.

When it was my turn, I fought back and thrashed my legs around. I was determined not to follow their orders.

"Hold still!" a guard said.

"I want to go to my mother."

"Hold still!"

"No, I want to see my mother. Bring me to my mother."

"You can see your mother . . . tomorrow. . . ." The man said that to calm me down. But I knew that I couldn't trust these people. They had separated us, why should they reunite us tomorrow? I thought, *There isn't much I can do to see my mother again, but I can cause a little trouble. As much as possible!*

Four people had to hold me down while they held the tip of an instrument similar to a fountain pen over an open flame and dipped it in blue ink. Then they held the hot needle against my skin and began to burn my registration number into the outside of my left arm: A-7063. I thrashed around so much that they couldn't manage to keep me still. Because I defended myself, the figures on my arm were blurred.

Miriam was different than me. She didn't fight back. Her number was A-7064. The lettering on her arm was completely clear. She was more like my father, complacent and calm, while I was more like my mother—always ready to put up a fight.

✶ ✶ ✶

In this short episode, a certain part of my personality emerged for the first time that had been unimportant up until then—my talent to think fast. In Auschwitz, there was no time to analyze things extensively or to make plans in order to then perhaps continue discussing plans. That's not how Auschwitz worked. Every action had to be carried out in seconds. If a piece of bread was lying there, forgotten, fallen, then the answer was to pick it up immediately, before someone else did. There was no time to stop and think. In addition, danger lurked everywhere. In every corner, from every direction.

That also meant there was never time to relax. Not for one second. Not even in my sleep. It was like on a battlefield, in the trenches, surrounded by allied and enemy soldiers.

Our barracks in Camp II B, the girl's camp in Birkenau, was also known as Auschwitz II. The building was a wooden stall that had originally been built for horses. Inside it was around eighty feet square and was bisected in the middle by a ledge of bricks. On each side of it was a walkway, which bordered the three-level bunk beds. In each bunk was a thin straw mattress and dirty sheet. Filled with children, between 200 and 500, from two to sixteen years old.

Everything inside here was covered in dirt. Lice were crawling everywhere, and there was no way to get rid of them. Their nests were in the mats, the straw, our clothing, everywhere. And there were entire hordes of rats. They were as big as cats. Uncommonly large. For me, as a ten-year-old, the rats were a huge problem since they looked terrifying.

When I saved a piece of bread in the evening so that I would have something to eat in the morning, the rats would eat it. No matter where I hid it. There was no place that they wouldn't find it. That's why the most important decision in the evening was: Do I want to eat everything, or do I want to hide it and risk having the rats find it? Theoretically, there was something to eat in the Nazi camps in the morning, but it often didn't materialize.

The size of the rats was unbelievable. I had seen rats before on our farm, but they were much smaller, and also much more timid. These lived blatantly in the barracks and were massive. I still don't understand why so little was written about these rats. They must have been seen and heard everywhere in Auschwitz; they were certainly looking for food in all the barracks since no one bothered to drive them away or even kill them.

The smell inside was even worse than the smell outside. In the lower portion of the barracks walls there were no windows to let in light or air, only above our heads, along the ceiling, which made it very stuffy.

At the end of the barracks, there was a latrine with three holes in the ground, another so-called privilege for twins. In the other barracks, they didn't even have that.

In retrospect, I have a better grasp of what happens when children are put in a situation as scary and unfamiliar as Auschwitz. When children are separated from everything they know and love, and instead are faced with death all of a sudden, they have to grow up extremely fast. They lose their childhood very fast.

These children who are confronted with life and death are no longer children. And I, too, lost my childhood in these first days. And it could never be returned to me.

✴ ✴ ✴

The food consisted of six-centimeter thick, extremely dark bread, which tasted like sawdust, and a brownish water that they called *Muckefuck* or coffee replacement in German. None of that was kosher.

I cannot remember exactly what my religious beliefs were when I was a little girl. But I knew through and through that God reigned over us, looked down on me and would punish me if I did bad things. My father had passed down this fear of God to us kids.

That's why I didn't want to eat the bread the first days. Although there wasn't anything else to eat. But Miriam and I refused the food because it wasn't kosher. For four days! I only drank the *Muckefuck*. It was not prepared in a kosher way, either, but the water had been boiled and therefore purified from some bacteria and impurities. In the camps, dysentery was widespread—a sickness that caused serious stomach infections and could even be fatal. The boiled *Muckefuck* water was the only water that was harmless. The water from the taps was filled with bacteria that caused typhus and diarrhea.

But soon I would have to throw my religious traditions overboard in order to survive.

In the afternoon, there was a sticky, very thick type of grain-based sludge to eat. The problem was that it was so thick you could neither chew nor swallow it. Later, I met some of the other twins and asked them how they were able to swallow it. And they all agreed with me—it wasn't edible.

On the very first evening, before we went to sleep, Miriam and I went to the latrine at the end of the barracks. I couldn't believe my eyes. Lying on the floor, in the filth, were the corpses of three children, their eyes open, their skin shriveled.

I carry this image with me even today. It is still as vivid as it was that night.

This moment may be partially responsible for making me who I am today. Because in that place, at that moment, I made a silent vow to do everything in my power so that Miriam and I wouldn't end like those children.

From the moment that we left the latrine, I concentrated all my efforts, all my thoughts on one thing—survival! From that moment on I held fast to the idea that we would both leave the camp alive. I never allowed fears or doubts to rule my thoughts again. As soon as they surfaced, I emphatically suppressed them. For it was a matter of surviving one more day in this horrible place.

Today, I am absolutely convinced that if I hadn't seen those dead children lying in the filth I wouldn't have lasted one month in the conditions in Auschwitz. We were already thin when we were brought there, but afterward there was hardly anything to eat. And more than that, we had lost our parents and our siblings.

We were children in an evil world.

⁕ ⁕ ⁕

In the morning, *"Auf! Auf! Auf!"* ("Up! Up! Up!") accompanied by a shrill whistle. That would follow us every morning from then on.

Outside the barracks, everything was dark, gray, lifeless. Threatening. I cannot recall that grass, trees, or flowers grew anywhere. Smoke hung over the entire camp. Fine ash filled the air, the sky, and darkened everything. The ash was so thick in the air; it was similar to the aftermath of a volcano eruption.

Some older people said, "If the Nazis think you are young and strong enough to live, they let you live. The others are packed into the gas chambers and gassed."

Hand in hand, we watched as the big girls helped the littler ones get ready for the roll call. As ten-year-olds, we were among the older ones. Some of the children were just two or three years old. They couldn't put on their shoes by themselves. Clothes weren't a problem since there was no fresh change of clothes. We always wore the same ones, day and night. The only things we possessed were the tatters on our bodies. And our lives. Only when the tatters couldn't be sewn together did we receive new prisoner's clothes. It was bare survival.

"Up, up, up!"

We assembled outside in lines of five and let ourselves be counted.

Each child had to be counted at roll call every day, whether living or dead. Dr. Mengele wanted to know how many twins he had, and no corpse was allowed to be disposed of without following exact regulations.

"Dr. Mengele is coming!" the SS guardswoman screamed. The guard personnel seemed nervous and uneasy, awaiting this important man.

Dr. Josef Mengele entered the barracks. He was elegantly dressed in an SS uniform, always immaculate, and wore high, shiny black riding boots. He had white gloves on and held a baton in his hand. An entourage of SS soldiers and other supervisors circulated around him. He was surrounded by an aura of absolute power.

Sometimes I look back at my behavior toward him back then. Although Mengele held our lives in his hand, I couldn't afford him any flattery—it was impossible. But we were at his mercy. In a certain way, he was both our torturer and our protector since as long as he needed us to live, we were allowed to live. Every single one of us understood that within just a few days.

Later, Dr. Münch would say again and again how Mengele told him, "I am protecting these twins. Without my experiments, they would all already be dead." That's how he could rationalize his deeds.

Mengele counted the twins in each bunk bed, followed by an entourage of eight people. He insisted that the gypsy girls in the neighboring barracks be dressed perfectly. He even distributed stockings. However, when their seams weren't lined up perfectly, he screamed at the nurses. He insisted on "picture-book" children. He acquired silk slippers for the gypsy boys. He also observed the little ones and asked them questions.

In October 1944, all the gypsies in the camp were murdered—the children together with their parents, all of them gassed.

In groups of five, we marched from Birkenau to the laboratories in Auschwitz. Mengele apparently wanted to figure out the secret to the formation of twins. The purpose of his experiments was finding out how to make large numbers of blond-haired, blue-eyed babies, in order to multiply the German population, the so-called "Aryans."

We entered a large, two-story brick building. Miriam and I were forced to take off our clothes, underwear, and shoes. There were boys and girls around us, all together in one room. Twenty or thirty pairs of twins.

None of us said a word.

While the SS guards pointed at us, laughing, we had to undress. The nakedness was the most degrading aspect for me in the camps. Dr. Mengele was always dropping by to check on things. Other doctors and nurses in white coats—prisoners of the camps, just like us—observed us or took notes. Everything proceeded with cool detachment, very methodically, and just the facts. Not an unnecessary word. Scientific, so to speak. And every scientist who carries out laboratory experiments comes into contact with the guinea pigs sooner or later. That was our relationship. We knew that we were alive because of the experiments. And they helped us stay alive. Our fate was in their hands.

First they measured my head. Then they measured my earlobes, the bridge of my nose, the width of my lips, the size, shape, and color of my eyes. And when they were done measuring, they compared it to Miriam's body. I was a nothing, a nobody. Only a collection of cells whose sole purpose was to be compared.

They took three to four hours to measure each ear. We were always naked. Every time the doctors measured me, they also considered Miriam and looked at their charts for a long time to figure out in which aspects we were identical and where we differed.

There were also technicians who took x-rays of us, sometimes five or six times in a row.

As a ten-year-old kid, you don't analyze what is happening to you here and now. Your only motivation is instinct: the will to survive. A ten-year-old child has limited mental energy. You don't think about what these people are saying in detail. It's just about survival. In these moments, I promised something to myself, and only myself—that Dr. Mengele and his helpers would never finish their job with us.

I will survive!

We sat there for six to eight hours at a time.

Like I said, we were the guinea pigs and it was made clear to us that they could do whatever they wanted to our bodies. In the service of a science that wanted to create the perfect race, the master race. We had no clue about genetics. We only knew that we weren't allowed to talk with the other prisoners. We had no idea what they put into or took from our bodies, and we had no influence over how they handled us. And we had no chance to escape it.

We were a control group, period. Nothing more than a small piece of a higher experiment. Useful because our birth had given rise to an interesting duality. Interesting for the sake of science. So there was no particular reason for the laboratory workers to be friendly to us. After all, we were just the guinea pigs.

Until today, none of us knows what exactly they did to us.

"You couldn't run away?"

Sometimes visitors to my Holocaust museum in Terre Haute ask me this question—they cannot even begin to imagine the conditions in Auschwitz. Run away? There was a barbed wire fence around the camp that was electrified twenty-four hours a day. The entire camp was surrounded by it. Before you could even reach the high-voltage fence, there was a stream. So whoever actually made it to the fence would have to first swim through the stream; as soon as you touched the fence with damp hands, you would immediately be electrocuted by the fence. And when I imagine actually making it past the fence, where could I have escaped to as a ten-year-old? Somewhere in the middle of nowhere . . .

The first two days, Miriam and I cried ceaselessly. But soon we realized that crying wouldn't help us at all.

Usually we felt numb. Staying alive was the most important thing. We knew that we were still alive because of the experiments. Because of a happy coincidence in nature.

Because we were Mengele's twins.

In retrospect, I think that it was important to have someone I could rely on: Miriam. And that she also had someone she could rely on.

There was one person who pulled me out of my isolation, and that was really important. In the meantime, there are now studies about how most people who have survived life-threatening situations were not utterly on their own but had someone they could hold onto, someone to support them. This shows that we humans cannot live in a vacuum, seemingly independent from other people. Even the majority of Auschwitz survivors I have talked with had an attachment person of some type. Or at least a hope that they could hold on to.

The whim of nature that made me born as a twin gave me both of these things.

I seldom thought about my parents and sisters. Somehow I sensed that there was a reason Miriam and I had been chosen to survive. And that my beloved mother was pushed into the row that led to the crematorium. And that my father and sisters were standing in the same group.

Of course I had no idea what happened to them. But some kind of protective mechanism in my mind that was meant to keep me from going crazy with longing somehow banished my family from my thoughts almost entirely. I had to cope with the fact that the two of us only had each other. Miriam and Eva.

⁎ ⁎ ⁎

In the morning, after roll call, before sunrise, in the darkness, Mengele came into our barracks for inspection. Smiling, he called us "my children." We stood there like statues. There was no conversation with him, no human interaction. Sometimes he brought cookies or chocolate for some of the youngest children. I never got sweets, and I think he didn't like me. Just as much as I didn't like him. I was defiant and rebellious.

After several days, we had to have our hair cut short after the roll call. We had head lice. They lived everywhere. Lice and fleas lived in our blankets, the straw mattresses, and our clothes. We scratched ceaselessly. Even with our shorn hair, we still had lice.

Once a week, twins had the so-called privilege of showering. Each of us got a piece of soap. We got undressed in a huge shower room and put our clothes in a stack to be disinfected. Later, I learned that the chemical used to disinfect our clothes, Zyklon B, was one of the three chemicals used to gas people in Auschwitz.

We got a new piece of soap to shower with every time. It was the only thing that wasn't scarce in Auschwitz. There was loads of soap in the stockrooms. But I never thought much about it.

Three days a week, they forced us to go to the laboratories of Auschwitz for intensive examinations that left us exhausted. On three other days, we were in the blood laboratories in Birkenau. Six days a week, we were guinea pigs.

The route there and back was also fenced in with barbed wire. Everything was a "restricted military area." If anyone got the notion to run away, then the sirens would go off in an instant and a troop of guards would be assembled. We were forced to stand in line for as long as it took to catch the escaped prisoner. Living or dead. That could take anywhere up to four hours.

If escapees were found alive, they were hanged immediately. Before our very eyes. The lesson we were to learn from that was obvious. If the person was found dead, they also displayed the corpse in front of us. One thing was clear; no one could escape Auschwitz.

Several years ago, I held a presentation in San Francisco to which other Auschwitz survivors were also invited. One of them recounted how he escaped from Auschwitz!

I was enthused. I told him excitedly that now I knew why I had had to endure so many long hours of waiting in the raiding party. I was so happy to know that someone had actually made it!

As for me, at ten years of age I wouldn't have thought about fleeing for one second. That was simply unthinkable. My only desire, every day, was simply to live another day. To survive another experiment. Every day.

In the blood laboratory, someone put thin, flexible rubber tourniquets on our left and right upper arms. Two people were working on me at the same time. One doctor stuck a needle in my left arm and drew blood. He took a full tube and then stuck me again.

At the same time, another doctor injected some substance into my right arm. He stuck five needles into my arm without removing the first. *What is he injecting into the rest of my blood?*

Our blood was taken until we lost consciousness.

I saw children who went blind because Mengele wanted to change their eye color. I saw children who were mutilated or who died after castration, amputation, or the removal of organs.

I was ten years old—but I refused to utter cries of pain because the Nazis shouldn't know that they were causing me pain. I managed to do so by turning my head away and counting the injections until they were finished.

We gave them our blood, our bodies, our pride, our value, and in turn they let us live another day.

We didn't know the purpose of the experiments or what they injected into us. Later I learned that Dr. Mengele purposely infected some of the twins with serious or even life-threatening illnesses, such as scarlet fever, and then injected them with all kinds of substances to see if they would cure the illness. In these investigations, I learned that cross-gender blood transfusions were also attempted. The blood from a boy would be injected into a girl, and vice versa. And back again. They didn't care whether the blood groups in the different bodies were compatible or not, so most of the twins died. One survivor, who lives in Israel today, told me in Jerusalem that she was subjected to such an experiment with her twin brother. Lying on the operating table, she realized that her brother suddenly became cold. He died.

She survived but has a number of health problems even today.

Another twin had his sexual organs removed in an attempt to change him from a boy into a girl.

Another girl had her uterus removed.

Some twins disappeared. Just like that. They told us the twins had become "very sick." Mengele simply replaced them with new pairs of twins. According to our research, there were 1,500 pairs of twins in Auschwitz, and presumably around 100 survived. Investigations revealed that almost all the twins died in the experiments. It was in fact very easy to die there. To be left to die in the barracks of death and to have survived it, as I did, was the absolute exception.

Not even Mengele's favorites were treated like humans. We were replaceable. Interchangeable.

However, I couldn't have pity on either myself or Miriam or on anyone else. I could never see myself as a victim; otherwise, I would die—I was sure of it. There was no space in me for any other thoughts except one: to survive.

If I had told Miriam how hungry or miserable I was, it would have just made everything worse.

That's why I didn't think about my family anymore. Presumably, I didn't think about anything. Today, I am not sure whether this void was a defense mechanism that helped me to cope with the terrible conditions, or whether—as some rumors claimed—it had to do with the bromine added to the food, a substance that stupefies, leads to memory loss, and weakens resistance.

⁕ ⁕ ⁕

Sometimes visitors to the museum ask if we made friends in Auschwitz. Impossible!

Our only thought: survival. The only rule: survival. There were no other thoughts, not even the prospect of wanting to think about something else. Even Miriam and I barely spoke with each other. Especially not about how we felt. And if we had talked about the terrible things at the camp, we would have died. The only exception was a short exchange to make sure she was more or less okay. That was important. But no details, please! That would have been an additional burden for me. My entire energy was focused on surviving—I was determined to leave that place alive. In every second. With every thought.

For visitors to the museum nowadays, I use a comparison that only roughly approximates the situation in Auschwitz but perhaps serves to illustrate. Imagine that you get a flat tire in the desert. No food, no water, no cell phone, no help. Your only thought is to send some kind of help signal. And you will not stop looking for help of any kind.

That is an intensity that one can hardly describe.

An incredibly lonely struggle.

Hope?

Our only hope in Auschwitz was to survive for just this moment (second). And to still be able to think more or less clearly. In other words, to think about how I can survive. Beyond that, there was constant oscillation between screams and terrifying silence. Thousands of people but no communication with each other. No smiling. No solidarity.

A lack of warmth.

Complete emotional isolation.

My exchanges with Miriam consisted mostly of "Do you have a piece of bread?" "Don't get sick."

Here is an example of the passivity that increasingly took the place of our feelings. It was a day on which we sat in front of our barracks. Lethargic. Silent. And suddenly several trucks drove by, carrying corpses. We ran to the fence to see if we could recognize anyone. Then one of the girls began to cry. "Mama, Mama, that is my mama," she screamed.

She wailed uncontrollably as the gravedigger drove past. In this moment, we all realized that our mothers might have also been carried off this way. We had never seen them again.

We were all stunned. But no one said anything to the little girl. Because no one could have put anything into words. We pitied her.

I wonder where my mother is, I thought to myself.

Ever since the first night, when I saw the smoking chimney, I hadn't thought about my mother anymore. It wasn't possible. In that first night I was convinced that my mother was dead, and at that moment, all thoughts about my family and my home had evaporated. Perhaps it was another defense mechanism. Or a result from the numbing substances in our food. Or it was my firm decision not to end up on the floor of the latrine, like the dead children.

But I knew at the same time that I couldn't torture myself with thoughts about death or other things I couldn't control. That was no way to survive.

I had to take care of myself—and Miriam.

Death meant ending up on the muddy floor of the latrine like a piece of rubbish or lying haphazardly on a wooden truck bed with the other bodies.

On this day, when the girl at the fence mourned for her mother, death became tangible. With this cart of corpses. But death was something I didn't want to come into contact with. This will was so strong in me that even when I became deathly ill shortly thereafter, I was able to renew my life-affirming decision.

I depended on this valuable life. My only thought was to resist death and stay alive.

And I knew I would survive. I just knew it. I just had to tell myself again and again: Just one more day. Just one more experiment. Just one more injection. And please, please, don't let us get sick.

One Saturday in July, they injected me with something that must have been a pathogen. They only gave me the shot, not my twin sister. Mengele stood on and observed everything with cold precision. That night, I developed a high fever. In the darkness, I heard a whistle, a car or motorcycle driving by. Marching sounds, moaning, vomiting, barking, and crying broke the silence of the camp. My head was pounding. My skin was burning and dry. My arms and legs swelled up. My body shivered so much that I couldn't sleep, despite my exhaustion. But the next morning I still had to go to roll call.

That's when something crucial happened. Right before the roll call actually started, the air raid sirens gave a loud, penetrating warning siren; we were being bombed. Trembling with joy, I watched the SS guards seek shelter while an airplane with American flags painted on the wings circled over the concentration camp.

That was the first airplane I had ever seen. It electrified me. I recognized the flag because an aunt lived there, but I had no idea how the world out there was made up or which countries there were. I had grown up in a village.

At the same time, roll call still started. Even with me, bright red with fever. There were no exceptions. Only death could save one from roll call. That's how the day started.

When I think back to that morning, I consider an interesting theory. What would have happened if, the whole time in the camp, the entire summer long, no airplane had flown over?

The American airplanes gave us hope. They signaled that someone we didn't know would free us. Even though we barely talked about it. *Hope!* For the first time, we kids developed a slogan: "Soon we will be free and can go home!"

If we could only stay alive long enough.

But we had no idea how this liberation would take place. There was no radio, no newspaper, no news about the world out there. I didn't even know whether the world still existed out there. A ten-year-old child cannot imagine that there are people who live in completely different conditions.

So, how long can a child or human being survive and fight without hope?

Without the airplane, without the bombs, many prisoners would have died of despair. Hope is a very important ingredient when you are fighting to survive. And those airplanes represented hope in a huge way.

Today I sometimes wish that the bombers had set their sights directly on the railway tracks. Many survivors talk about this because it would have held up the transports for a while. Many, many people's lives could have been saved by a single bomb. The pilots didn't do it, and I cannot change that. But it makes me sad to think that they didn't even try.

* * *

My fever rose continually. In the laboratory, they measured my temperature. I realized that I was in trouble.

The nurses brought me to Hospital Block 21, a filthy barracks close to the gas chamber and the blazing chimneys.

I remember reading about the "valley of the shadow of death" in the Bible. That's how I felt.

We received no food rations. Another patient said, "Because they bring people here to die or be transferred from here to die in the gas chambers."

I am not allowed to die, I ordered myself.

I will not die!

In the morning after my arrival, Mengele visited me with a team of four other doctors. They discussed my case as if I were in a normal hospital.

Dr. Mengele laughed and said with an ironic grin, "What a shame. She is so young and has just two weeks to live."

Only later did I find out that Mengele knew which illness they had infected me with and how it would progress. It could have been typhus or beriberi.

But in that instant, without having to consciously prompt myself, the thought welled up in me, *I will show you that you are wrong!*

Even today I don't know where my certainty came from.

I will survive with my sister! I didn't want to simply try to do so—no, I would survive!

I told myself, "I am not dead. I refuse to die. I will punish Dr. Mengele for his lies and come out of here alive."

In fact, I never imagined myself dying, not even once. I could picture in my mind how Miriam and I would walk out of the camp.

In the following days, I had a sustained, very high fever, but no one gave me food, medication, or water. They only checked my temperature. I was so thirsty; I had such a dry mouth that I didn't think I could breathe for much longer.

At the other end of the infirmary barracks was a water faucet. I remember sliding out of bed, opening the door, and crawling across the floor to reach this sink. I needed water desperately, even though I knew it could be full of bacteria. I reached out my hands and dragged my body along on all fours, crawling slowly across the floor, which was covered with excrement and filth. From time to time, I lost consciousness, then I came to and pushed myself forward, inch by inch.

I will get well, I repeated ceaselessly to myself.

I must live. I must survive.

That was the only thing that enabled me to survive: my will. And a little luck.

The will alone is not always enough.

I don't even know how I made it back into my bunk bed in that room each time. And yet I dragged myself to that water faucet every night for two weeks. And back again.

Every night.

The need for water surpassed everything else. The worst part is I don't actually remember drinking water. But I must have since that was the only way I could have survived.

After my first week in the infirmary, Miriam found out that I was getting absolutely nothing to eat. Then she began saving bread for me and passed it on to an acquaintance, Mrs. Csengeri, who was also imprisoned in the camp with her twin daughters, so that she could secretly give it to me.

What dedication, what willpower—a ten-year-old who decides not to eat anything for a week! This piece of bread each day from my sister helped save my life, and it fueled my determination to return to Miriam.

After two weeks, as if by a miracle, my fever went down.

How I survived remains a mystery to me to this day. I am not a religious person, so I cannot fall back on the explanation that a guardian angel or some other deity intervened in my life—but I have no other explanation. There is no logical way to justify how I could have survived without medicine, completely malnourished and dehydrated. No one took care of me. There was no communication. To this day, I don't even know how I found that water faucet. Surrounded by deathly ill people who couldn't care less whether or not one of the others survived. Because they had been left for dead themselves.

Nevertheless, I never imagined myself dead. Not even once. There was this image firmly etched in my mind of me leaving the infirmary. Surrounded by death and despair, I don't know where I got this inspiration.

But I was released.

Afterward, I didn't say, "Thank you" to Miriam. That's the way it was in the camp. There was no room for such words there. And no time. Miriam had become sick herself.

✳ ✳ ✳

The first time we talked about it was in 1985. Out of nowhere, she asked me, "Did you ever get the bread that I saved up for you?"

In 1985, for the first time, I thanked her for it.

Since then, I have often wondered, *What is it that allows us to stay human?* I think it is the will to do everything for another person. Without expecting anything in return, not even a simple "thank you."

I saw many people in Auschwitz who had to survive completely alone, but they vegetated in a dark state of consciousness. Almost like animals. There was no one whose company they could share. Even worse, every trace of humanity had disappeared. These poor beings just barely functioned somehow. And they survived this way—without humanity, afraid, filled with pain and anger.

In Auschwitz, after my surprising recovery and my return from the infirmary, I saw Miriam again, and her appearance horrified me. She had an empty expression in her eyes; she simply sat there and stared into space. She seemed weak and apathetic.

I realized how seriously our separation had impacted Miriam. The idea of being completely alone had destroyed her hope. In camp language, she had become a *Muselmann*, a living corpse. A being who felt no motivation at all to fight for her life.

Never, never, absolutely never give up!

That's the only way for me.

And that is my lesson from Auschwitz. Since giving up in Auschwitz would have meant certain death. There were these people, the *Muselmänner*, sick, who just sat on their wooden beds, crouched on the floor, and stared at the ceiling, at the sky. Nothing more in them, no desires, no feelings, no more interest in living.

That was exactly how my sister looked. She had given up. She was skin and bones. There was no spirit left in her, no consciousness.

I had to ignite a light in her.

Later I learned that Miriam had been taken to a laboratory a few days previously. When I didn't die as Mengele had expected, they took Miriam and injected her with several shots to make her ill. The injections stopped the growth of her kidneys, so that they remained the size of a ten-year-old's kidneys. I never found out the purpose of these experiments on my sister.

Through my research, I was only able to find out that Mengele had suffered from kidney problems when he was sixteen. According to his SS file, he missed three to four months of school because of health issues. He was very interested in the way the kidneys functioned. I am aware of three cases in which

Mengele's twins were infected with different kidney diseases, and they still don't respond to antibiotic treatment, even today.

In addition, I learned that Mengele—who had planned my death with an injected disease—contracted pathologists on a regular basis to carry out autopsies on twins who died within hours of each other. For him, it was a unique opportunity to investigate the effects of diseases by comparing diseased bodies to healthy ones that were otherwise almost completely identical.

If I had died in the infirmary, they would have brought Miriam to the laboratory immediately and killed her with a chloroform injection to the heart. Then they would have compared my diseased organs to her healthy organs in simultaneous autopsies. Now Miriam was seriously ill, with more than the ceaseless diarrhea caused by dysentery. Whereas we all suffered from that, Miriam had completely lost the will to live. I had to find a way to help spur her recovery.

In the camp, people said that potatoes strengthened you and were effective against diarrhea. But to even consider acquiring a food like that was unthinkable. Potatoes in Auschwitz! That was impossible, at least if you followed the rules.

That type of food could only be *organized*. In the language of the camp, that meant stealing it from the Nazis.

However, every person who was caught stealing would be hanged. At least we had heard of such executions. But I would inevitably have to take the risk for Miriam. I couldn't let her die.

Some of the other twins told me that the only place to get potatoes was from the kitchen, which is why I volunteered to bring out the food. After morning roll call, I stood on my tiptoes, demonstrated loudly, jumped up and down, and made myself conspicuous in every way possible. Almost every prisoner wanted to work in the kitchen. So I had to call more loudly than the others. Until I finally succeeded.

That's how I became one of two helpers who had to drag a huge container of soup, as big as a 100-liter garbage container, from the kitchen to the end of the camp, to our barracks. On foot, the distance was about a twenty-minute walk normally. But now two kids were dragging the soup container.

I had barely stepped into the kitchen when I saw a long metal table with pots and pans. Underneath it, I discovered two sacks of potatoes. I hesitated for an instant. If I was caught, they would hang me—that was an unwritten law. But if I didn't try, Miriam would die.

I bent down and looked around to see if anyone was watching me. While my heart was pumping so hard that I could feel the blood in my ears, I gathered all my courage, reached into the sack and grabbed two potatoes.

All of a sudden, someone grabbed me by the head and pulled me up. It was the kitchen worker, a fat prisoner with a striped towel around his head.

"It's not nice to steal!"

What? It's not *nice* to steal? I had assumed I would be hanged. I let the potatoes fall back into the sack. I still expected to be dragged from the kitchen to the gallows, but that didn't happen.

I had just learned that being one of Mengele's twins also meant that no one dared to intentionally hurt us—as long as Mengele wanted us alive.

The next day, I stood up on my tiptoes again, raised my hands, volunteered loudly and was taken for kitchen duty again.

However, this time it was easier to organize potatoes without being caught. As soon as I was close to the sacks, I quickly reached under the table and hid three potatoes under my dress. Every other secret activity, including cooking, would have to happen later. At night. One of the twin girls brought a few coals that she had organized during the day. At the end of the brick ledge that bisected the barracks, we started a little fire in the oven.

This was of course also strictly forbidden. So one of the kids stood watch and signaled if a guard was approaching by tapping their feet. That was also touching; although we were all skin and bones, and it was often only our hunger that reminded us we were still alive, we didn't try to take food away from one another.

I cooked three potatoes with the peel, buds, and dirt crust, but they were delicious. Miriam and I had a feast. We ate the potatoes without salt or butter, but they tasted fantastic. They filled us with warmth and lifted our spirits.

I got better at organizing each time. I took a few more potatoes than we needed each time, so Miriam and I often had potatoes three days in the space of a week.

The food I organized for Miriam was indeed as effective as medicine. Her health improved, she regained her strength and was once again prepared to fight for her life. Vice versa, taking care of Miriam also helped me become stronger and more robust. Miriam's life was my task and purpose in life.

In Auschwitz it was so easy to die. Surviving was harder—it was hard work.

✳ ✳ ✳

In late summer of 1944, more and more planes zoomed past overhead and bombed the command posts and factories of the Nazis. At this point in time, our liberation was no longer a hypothetical question—it was palpable everywhere.

Freedom!

We could hear freedom. We could see it. It couldn't be much longer until our liberation. There were isolated rumors that the SS would kill everyone imprisoned in the camp while the Allies—the armies of the Americans, Brits, and Soviets—were approaching.

Seemingly unfazed, Dr. Mengele continued his experiments. However, he seemed nervous and lost in his thoughts when I saw him for the last time. That wasn't good, for when he was nervous, he was prone to fits of madness. There had been unexpected deaths among the twins, and he was ranting and screaming a lot because of it.

The rumors were multiplying that we would be the next to be gassed. But first, the routine continued. Mercilessly. And no matter how many airplanes blared above us—each morning there was still roll call. And if need be, we would even stand several hours outside in the cold. Day in and day out.

Meanwhile, airplanes were circling around us. And we could hear explosions. Everywhere. Every morning.

In October 1944, during one roll call there was suddenly a gigantic explosion in one of the crematoriums. Back then we couldn't comprehend what was going on. A beacon. A symbol, in retrospect. Only years later was it revealed that it had been a revolt of the so-called *Sonderkommando* (special unit), which had decided it was better to die fighting than to be killed silently. Its members were Jewish work prisoners whose task was to prepare the murder of fellow deported prisoners and to subsequently burn their corpses in the crematorium.

Shortly after this revolt, the Nazi headquarters decided that no more Jews were to be gassed in Auschwitz—a detail we were unaware of.

We assumed that we would die. The Nazis had just wiped out the gypsy camp, and now we were supposed to move into their barracks. The rumors were clear, we would be next. So we marched over to our camp, and on the first day in the new barracks we were supposed to appear at roll call immediately. But this time from five in the morning to four in the afternoon.

It was the longest roll call ever. It had become extremely cold; it was autumn, and the ground was frozen. One of my feet had frostbite, and the same happened to Miriam. However, my sister never really recovered from this frostbite; she had problems with that foot for the rest of her life.

Today I still don't know why we were counted for so long that day, and why we were transferred in the first place. But now we lived in the shadow of the crematorium.

⁕ ⁕ ⁕

From November 1944, the experiments stopped all of a sudden. There were too many bombings, artillery was blaring everywhere. Dr. Münch would later recount that Mengele packed his files, loaded them into a car, and left Auschwitz a few weeks later. Only loose, single pages from his notes were later found there.

In early January 1945, more and more people had to leave the barracks at the orders of the SS and were sent on forced marches. "Out, out!" they screamed. "Everyone out!"

The official reason for the marches was to protect us from the battles. "I will not leave the barracks," I told Miriam. "I am not going on a march."

I had loathed the Nazis when they were about to win the war, and now that they were losing the war, they were bound to become even more horrible. So we hid.

We lay down, slept, and awoke in stillness.

Unfamiliar stillness.

To my astonishment, no one came and picked us up. The SS soldiers had been in such a rush to drive everyone out that they hadn't bothered to check every single barracks. One set of twins stayed back with us.

From the 150,000 people who had lived in Birkenau, there were maybe 8,000 left. All of the guards, commanders, and dogs, all of the cries and commands that had characterized our everyday life had suddenly disappeared. At least it seemed to be the case.

I spent my time searching for food, water, and blankets in order to keep my sister and myself alive. Food was like medicine for Miriam. Otherwise, we had no medical care. Food was our only hope.

Together with another girl, I went to the place where the Nazis kept all the clothing, shoes, and blankets they had taken away from the prisoners. It was a building as big as a gym hall, filled with shoes, clothing, pants, jackets—with everything. The Nazis had called this building "Canada."

I rummaged through shoe after shoe, but I found none that fit. There were hardly any kids my age there, so I finally chose a pair two sizes too big for me. I stuffed scraps of fabric into the toes of the shoes and wrapped a string around each shoe.

Miriam's shoes were in better shape because she wasn't out and about as I was to organize food and clothing. It was very, very cold, and we needed warm clothing desperately.

The following afternoon, I crept into the kitchen to organize more bread. Then I heard the strange sound of a car.

An off-road military vehicle hurtled toward the building, and four Nazis with machine guns jumped out and began firing in all directions.

In a split second, I saw the muzzle of a gun being pointed at my head, just a few feet away from me—that's nothing, just a little more than two or three arm lengths away—and then I lost consciousness.

When I came to, I thought, *Aha, now I must be dead.* I was certain that I was on the other side. *So that's what it looks like in the afterlife.* Corpses were lying all around me.

Then I moved my arms. I moved my legs. I touched the person next to me, a girl, but she didn't move. Her body was cold. *Why?* She was dead, all the people around me were dead—but I was alive.

Sometimes I think today that it must have been fate—fate that I didn't die at that very moment. How could a bullet possibly miss me from such a short distance? How could it be that at the exact moment they took aim at me, I fainted?

On the other hand it also makes me sad since all the dead people around me were so close to being liberated. So close! And they were all killed. Why did the Nazis return in the first place?

The following night, there was an explanation. We were awakened by smoke and heat, and flames shot down from the roof. We felt the searing heat of the fire through the barracks walls. The buildings were on fire! We grabbed our things and ran outside. The Nazis were back, they were no longer in hiding, and they were presumably trying to destroy the evidence of their crimes. The sky was red from the glow of the flames as far as we could see. The SS had set another crematorium and "Canada" on fire. Countless pieces of clothing flew through the air.

At the same time, the Allies attacked again, and bombs lit up the sky. It seemed as if the entire world was in flames. Thousands of people streamed out of the endless rows of barracks. The same SS soldiers I had seen near the kitchen were now rounding us up for our departure.

And this time we couldn't flee.

I held Miriam's hand tightly.

It seemed to me we'd have the best chances if we didn't walk at the beginning or the end of the crowd but somewhere in the middle. Which wasn't easy.

The SS fired again and again at random into the crowd, while they herded us together. All around us, people fell dead to the ground. Our fear grew. Even the children and elderly, who had been spared from previous marches, had to join this time.

Later, we found out that 8,200 had people left Birkenau with us that night. Along the way, within a single hour 1,200 of them were killed.

In the middle of the night, we finally reached the barracks of Auschwitz. The brick buildings glowed in the light of the sunlamps.

However, the SS guards had inexplicably disappeared. All of a sudden, they were gone. Without any orders being given.

In all the chaos, I lost my twin sister. Miriam was gone! I panicked.

But no matter how loudly I screamed, I couldn't find her.

Many of the fellow prisoners couldn't care less about my desperation. They were at the end of their rope, too. There wasn't a single gram of empathy left for someone else. "You are looking for your sister? So what? I have absolutely no one. . . ."

But Miriam was more than a sister for me—she was my second self. Our collective survival depended on us being together.

I looked for Miriam for over twenty-four hours, but to no avail. But she couldn't have simply disappeared.

What I couldn't know at the time was that Miriam had looked for me nonstop. We were continually crossing paths and missing each other.

When we were finally reunited, she held a piece of chocolate in her hand. That was the moment we decided to hold hands whenever possible. So that we could never be separated again.

The following days, Miriam and I had to rely on ourselves.

My daily task was to find something to eat for both of us. She was in poor condition. I tended to run around, nervous and jittery, and I wouldn't accept any failure. It was easier for me to cope with the change.

In the buildings where the SS had lived, we found lots of food on the tables. There were rumors that the food was possibly poisoned, as it had been arranged in such a conspicuous way. So we left it alone. But we found numerous containers of sauerkraut. There was loads of it. So from then on we ate sauerkraut and drank the juice. We even mixed the sauerkraut with jam for dessert. There was no clean water, and there was no snow, so sauerkraut juice was the only safe liquid to drink.

But there was one problem—we had had so little to eat the whole time in the camp, and now we were stuffing ourselves with anything that was more or less digestible. From morning to night. Most of us had swollen stomachs. Today I know how dangerous that is. When you have had barely anything to eat and then suddenly start to feast, then you swell up—and die.

In fact, some of our fellow prisoners died during this time, including people I had grown very fond of since we organized food together each day.

⁂ ⁂ ⁂

One morning, another pair of twins and I set off for the Weichsel River, which wasn't far from the camp. In the meantime, we had found enough bread but nothing to drink. Armed with a few bottles and containers, we wanted to break the ice there, lower our bottles, and fill them with fresh water.

As I stood at the banks of the river, outside of the camp, I saw a girl my age on the other side. She wore her hair in braids and had a pretty, clean dress on, and a coat. She was wearing a school satchel on her back.

I froze. It was a vision, almost like something in a fairy tale. I couldn't imagine that there was still a world out there in which people were clean and girls wore braids with ribbons and nice dresses and went to school.

Up until this moment, I had somehow imagined that everyone lived in a concentration camp, like we did. But now I realized that wasn't the case. In retrospect, I think that the notion that everyone lived in a camp was a part of my survival strategy. I could only think about the here and now, about the struggle for survival, which was difficult enough.

But there, at the river, a girl was staring at me.

I wore tattered clothing, which was covered in lice, and a coat and shoes, all of which were far too big for me. I was hungry and had to look everywhere to find food and water.

We broke the ice, and as I raised my head and looked at the girl again, I felt something hot well up in me. Anger, rage. I felt deceived. Miriam and I had done no wrong! We were two little girls, just like she was. Why were we stuck in this camp, full of lice and disease, while on the other side she was so pretty and neat and could lead a completely normal life?

It was so incomprehensible for me, so wrong. But there she was. And here I was. After what felt like an eternity, she left.

The image of the girl remained etched into my mind—along with all my questions about the world out there.

We couldn't leave the camp because the battles were erupting all around us. We found ourselves in the middle of a combat zone.

Nevertheless, I crept to the riverbank every day and looked for the girl in the pretty dress. But she never returned.

Gunfire sprayed and rattled from the bunkers in which the SS had hidden after they left us in the barracks. We had learned how to evade the gunshots. They made a very specific, whining sound, and you had to take cover immediately since it meant bullets were flying in our direction. At this time, they were shooting around indiscriminately, and everyone and everything in the way could get shot.

For about nine days, we heard shots and bomb explosions continuously. Day and night. We were all talking about how we would soon be liberated. And on the morning of January 27, 1945, the noise suddenly ceased. For the first time in weeks, it was completely silent. The silence was almost spookier than the noise.

It snowed heavily. Then, around three or four in the afternoon, a woman came running into the barracks and started to shout in a shrill voice, "We are free! We are free!" Giant snowflakes floated down on me.

* * *

It had snowed all day long, and the dirty gray of Auschwitz was now covered in a white blanket of snow.

I couldn't see a thing. What did that mean, *Freedom?* How could you recognize it? It was snowing.

I stared into the distance. Around sixty meters away, men suddenly emerged from the white void, also draped in white, who were slowly marching toward us. They didn't speak, their boots crunched through the snow. Who were these men?

But they were smiling.

One thing was certain; they weren't Nazis. We ran to them, and they gave us cookies and chocolate. That was my first foretaste of freedom.

And then I knew that my silent oath, the oath I had made in the latrine that first night, that I had made again and again—that I wanted to survive and leave the camp alive with Miriam at my side—had become reality.

We were free!

What a magical word. What an overwhelming power these letters carry.

That was the only thing I had talked about in the last two or three months. "When we are finally free, we will go home." Now the moment had come. Now the longing for my family, which had been suppressed so long by my daily fight for survival, broke through. I hoped to actually find my mother and father and my sisters, and all I wanted was to go home. For I had survived.

2

I Was a Model Victim

From that point on, we danced—wildly.

A Ukrainian unit of the Soviet Army had freed us, and we celebrated with them in one of the barracks. Vodka flowed freely from the bottle directly into people's mouths, since there were no glasses, no more rules, and no fear. Everyone was laughing and singing, sitting on the ground, and jumping through the rooms. Someone played accordion.

All around us, people were in such high spirits and euphoria, which I have rarely seen since. And we enjoyed every second. There was so much joy in being alive. *We could do whatever we want*, I thought. Everything we wanted.

We are free.

✶ ✶ ✶

After three days, the men disappeared as suddenly as the Nazis had previously. We were worried.

Alone in the camp. The silence.

For three days, we looked uneasily into the distance.

But the men reappeared, this time carrying huge film equipment to reconstruct the liberation. They posted cameras, spotlights, and tripods along the paths; you didn't just carry this type of equipment around with you in wartime.

Then we were asked to put on prisoners' uniforms. This suggestion dampened our mood since we twins had never had to wear these uniforms. It was one of our so-called privileges. That's why some of us didn't want to put on the uniform. But in the end we played along. And when I see this propaganda film of the liberation today, with Miriam and I in the first row, with our confused, curious eyes, which seem a little foreign to me, I have the feeling that we are the most orderly kids in the whole troop.

"Home", I was saying at the time. "I want to go home."

Miriam looked at me for a long time. "Good. We are free. Let's go home."

"Where is that?" The older people in the liberated camp asked.

"In Romania."

"And how do you want to get there?"

Silence.

We had no idea. But I knew we had to go home. Miriam and I had already stowed all of our belongings under our coats and dresses—food, bowls, blankets—all of the things we considered to be our treasures; they were supposed to help us go home. But how?

I didn't even know which direction we were supposed to go. I didn't know where we were in the first place, let alone that there were different political systems. And that countries like

Poland or Romania were now Communist. And that our world was continually in upheaval. I only knew that I wanted to go home, in the childish hope that everything would return to the way it had once been.

First, a horse and cart took us to an orphanage in a Katowice monastery, where Miriam and I had a pretty, shared room. It was the only possible safe haven. No one knew what else they should do with us. We were two eleven-year-old girls without parents. Two beds were in the room, with fresh, white sheets. Fresh, white sheets! That was a sight I hadn't beheld in what seemed like an eternity.

We were dirty and covered in lice. *I can't possibly sleep in a clean, white bed like this*, I thought. So I pulled the sheets off the bed and lay down on the bare mattress. I didn't want to get everything dirty.

Otherwise, I was silent.

There were no words for what happened in the ten months since I had been torn away from my home. There was only longing—the longing that burns in every person, everywhere in the world, in every culture and language, when your world has been shattered and your heart as well; longing for the love of a mother and the feeling of security and familiarity that home brings.

The nuns were nice, perhaps somewhat naive, and they gave us toys and children's playthings. Miriam and I had since turned eleven, and our childhood had been taken from us in Auschwitz. We couldn't play with dolls and braid hair all of a sudden. And we would never play again, either; I never played with toys again in my life.

"We want to go home," we told the nuns.

"Where are your parents?" they asked.

"I don't know."

And after a short break, "We want to go home."

This conversation repeated itself day in and day out.

Somehow we found out that several Auschwitz survivors lived in a refugee camp in Katowice, including Mrs. Csengeri, with her twin daughters.

We knew her from home.

That's where we wanted to go.

Back then, we could ride the bus for free when we showed our Auschwitz tattoos. Sometimes we spent the whole day riding back and forth.

I finally found Mrs. Csengeri, put my hand on her arm, and said, "During our time in Auschwitz, I never asked you for anything. I know that you came to our barracks every day to give bread to your twins, and I understand you just didn't have enough for all of us."

She was silent.

"Mrs. Csengeri, could you please go to the monastery with us and sign some papers explaining you are our aunt?"

Without considering it for very long or even hesitating, she followed us, signed the papers and took us with her.

We lived with her and her children for nine months, nine months without worrying about where we would find something to eat or drink. And full of hope that we would be home soon.

In March 1945, Mrs. Csengeri woke me from a deep sleep. "Pack everything," she said. "We're leaving." It was early in the morning, but that was all I longed for—to finally go home.

We took the first train, followed by other trains, going toward Transylvania. Along the way, we stayed at displaced persons camps until we finally, finally reached our village after a strenuous week. We had returned to Portz.

In my mind, the idea of home consisted of Miriam and I, our sisters and our parents, our farm and animals. I excluded the possibility that this home may no longer exist. I blocked out even the faintest notion of this.

We held hands and walked through the village. It was the same route we had walked back then, when they took us away. I was still wearing the shoes from the camp, which were twice the size of my feet. And, just like back then, we were being watched. People whispered. They stared at us as we walked down the street. But no one spoke to us.

Then we saw our house.

Or at least what remained of our house.

It wasn't much. Hardly more than the unbuilt farmland and the bare walls of an empty building.

That was the moment when Miriam and I recognized that we were the only members of the Mozes family who had survived.

I don't know how long we stood there, silent, motionless, empty.

And through the emptiness, I could suddenly see my mother; her gaze was full of despair, with one arm reaching out to me and Miriam, although we were long since out of reach—on the selection ramp of Auschwitz.

We were alone.

⁂ ⋆ ⋆

The house was filthy from floor to ceiling, and it was otherwise empty. Everything had been stolen; the furniture, curtains, the dishes, every table, simply everything that was still usable to some extent.

I only found three photos, which were crumpled up on the wooden floor. I picked them up and kept them.

One of them is the last photo of my entire family, taken in autumn 1943. In the black-and-white photo, Miriam and I were wearing our identical wine-red dresses.

We spent several hours in the ruins.

Some of the villagers stood in front of their houses and continued to watch us silently. No one approached us. I was angry at the people, at their silence, this coldness. But I didn't say anything.

Miriam and I lived with Aunt Irena for the next five years, from 1945 to 1950. She owned a large apartment building in Cluj. She had also survived the Nazis. However, her husband and son had disappeared. Afterward, Irena married another man who had also lost his family.

But the big apartment building was meaningless now; on the contrary—Romania was now ruled by Communists, and large houses were considered to be a declaration of war against the people. The secret police often took over people's property and distributed it among the farmers. This menacing atmosphere, which made you feel powerless, reminded me of the era of National Socialism in many ways. I can still remember standing in line for five hours for just a piece of bread. Inflation rose by the hour, so that by the time I had finally reached the front of the line, the people in the shop had decided not to sell any more bread.

That day, I went back home and there was nothing to eat. There wasn't any food for the rest of the week. We just couldn't find anything edible. The government was in a hurry to pass a currency reform. But that was not enough. The food prices continued to rise. And people's stomachs were growling.

Nevertheless, the Communists had wonderful slogans, truly captivating slogans that announced equality, justice, and prosperity, but all of them were untrue. For example, we were not treated equally. Miriam and I were orphans—that's why they didn't arrest us, which could happen to any young person at that time, to be "reeducated" by the secret police with cruel torture. But I still never felt safe.

And we were not a real family. We all lived together, and we knew that our aunt cared about us; she was the only one of our relatives who was willing to take us in. But Aunt Irena didn't hug or kiss us, she never said anything loving to us. Still, Miriam and I were hungry for affection; we yearned for a loving mother.

Moreover, I had nightmares every night. I was plagued by rats biting me, rats as big as cats, and I dreamed about corpses and of needles being stuck into me.

One day, a rabbi in the synagogue asked us to bring the pieces of soap we had taken from the concentration camp for a memorial service. I didn't understand why, but I brought two pieces of soap—and found out. During the war, you couldn't get soap anywhere, except in Auschwitz. But we were told that the soap that we had used there constantly was made of human fat.

These nightmares haunted me for several years. First, I was horrified that I had potentially washed myself with soap that had been made from my parents. I had dreams in which pieces of soap spoke to me with the voices of my parents and sisters and they asked, "Why are you washing yourself with us?" Terrible! I told no one about it, not even Miriam. What could she have done about it? For several years I was still scared to wash myself with soap.

Otherwise we both had health issues and were constantly catching colds. But there was no doctor in the wider area. My teeth were rotten, I had painful sores on my hands that swelled to the size of apples and left scars. It was certainly an infection—but there were no antibiotics. And we had very little to eat. When Aunt Irene finally took us to a doctor in the next biggest city, I was overcome by fear and terror—I was reminded of Dr. Mengele and his assistants in their white coats.

"That is all caused by malnutrition," the doctor said. "The children are lacking in nothing which vitamins and nutritious food cannot alleviate."

But that's exactly what was unavailable at the time. Food was scarce, and one could only dream of vitamins.

Our cousin, Shmilu, once brought us flour, potatoes, eggs, vegetables, and sunflower oil from a farm. Miriam and I were crazy about the oil, we even drank it straight out of the bottle. My aunt was quite alarmed. "Children, what are you doing?" She even contacted the doctor about it, but he said she should let us drink the oil. It seemed that there was an ingredient in the oil that our bodies needed in order to recover. Otherwise, it would have been impossible to tolerate drinking that much oil at once.

We were also going to school again.

Miriam and I had missed a year and a half, but we weren't too far behind in the curriculum. School was still difficult for the two of us since our native language was Hungarian and the lessons were taught in Romanian. We caught up quickly together, and by the third year we were at the top of our class.

It was soon apparent that Miriam was the cautious, quiet one. I was always full of enthusiasm.

Miriam's strength was talking to the other survivors. She could empathize with other people easily, and the other survivors loved her dearly. That couldn't even be shaken by the fact that she was related to me, who saw no reason to not only continually revisit one's own horrible memories, but also the horrible recollections of others—it was heartbreaking.

At the same time, life in the Communist regime was getting harder and harder. The government controlled everything, including the schools. I even joined the Party and was promoted until I became responsible for thirty young pioneers. In 1948, there was a morning parade, with breakfast afterward, and during the parade I was informed that another strenuous parade was planned for that afternoon. I thought to myself, *No, that is a little too much marching for one day*. I still wanted to study, and the other children had to catch up on school work. So I sent them all home.

The next day, I was promptly summoned to the Communist Party headquarters. I told myself, "I am an Auschwitz survivor, what else could I possibly fear now?"

The local head of the party began by saying, "It has reached my ears that you consider learning to be more important than the work for the Communist Party. Remember one thing: you are not authorized to think. Your job is to carry out orders." This speech was accompanied by heavy blows to the table.

I was fourteen years old.

"That is alright," I replied. "If I am not allowed to think, then I don't want to belong to the Party anymore."

"Then we will exclude you," the man countered sharply.

My school career, that much I knew, would be damaged if I did so. Probably even more than that. So I nodded and remained in the Party. But from then on I didn't participate at all.

Aunt Irena said later that evening, "No one gets into trouble as quickly as you do, Eva. You have problems constantly."

⋆ ⋆ ⋆

We were the only Jews in the girls' high school. Other pupils insulted us despite everything we had been through.

So we listened up when the State of Israel was declared in Palestine in 1948. It was the place where my father had dreamed of taking refuge. And we had promised him to emigrate there. *If any of you survives this terrible war . . .*

Aunt Irena also wanted to emigrate. We applied for an exit visa for the three of us, and our aunt received hers without a hitch. But Miriam and I were put through additional inquiries, corrections, empty promises, and cancellations. The government simply wanted to prevent young people from leaving Romania since they needed young people to help rebuild the country after it had been devastated in the war. It took two whole years before we finally held our visa in our hands. Two years in which we were constantly bullied around.

In 1950, when we were finally ready to leave, the government informed us that we could only take the clothes on our backs. That wasn't much. So under our identical coats, we each wore three dresses. And that was in the middle of July, in midsummer. I had stood in line for more than twenty hours waiting for these coats, and I didn't want to leave them behind.

In addition, another condition of our emigration stipulated that we had to transfer our entire land, including the house and the stalls, to the government, and we had no other choice than to give away everything.

The only thing I took with me were the crumpled photos of my family, which I carefully wrapped in paper and stowed deep in my coat pockets.

I looked at them two or three times, and then didn't see them again for another twenty years. I didn't even think about them. The prospect of finally being free, and the determination to rebuild my life and make a home there apparently activated a psychological defense mechanism in me that protected me from my childhood memories. And the wounds on my soul, which would otherwise be reopened again and again.

✶ ✶ ✶

I was sixteen years old as I breathed in the salty air of the harbor city of Haifa. Finally, I was free—in Israel.

With three layers of dresses, a winter coat, and first and foremost—hope. And a pinch of relief that all the horror was behind us.

And it was indeed the case. Our Uncle Aaron, our father's brother, greeted us as we came ashore.

We worked part-time in our village and went to school the rest of the time. My job was to harvest the tomatoes and peanuts and to milk the cows.

At this time, I was filled with hatred of the Germans.

"And what happens now?" A friend asked me.

"What do you mean?"

"What will you do with your hate?" she replied.

I was silent. On one hand, I didn't know how to respond, but I also didn't want to change. But something was set into motion inside me.

"Do something about it," my friend said.

For the first time since I had left Auschwitz, I could sleep without nightmares. For the first time I felt safe. I didn't have to fear for our physical safety or our survival. Here there was no anti-Semitism, and we were allowed to—even encouraged to—celebrate our Jewish heritage. In these youth villages, our pain and wounds began to heal slowly. It happened in stages, for our physical rehabilitation went much faster than our psychological recovery.

⁂

Upon our arrival, we all spoke different languages, but we were taught a common language: Hebrew.

Otherwise, I learned songs and dances. Singing and dancing has been an expression of happiness for me ever since. That is also the reason why even today, at over eighty years old, I still want to dance the hora when I'm in a room with sad people. Back then, as a sixteen-year-old girl, simply jumping around, dancing and singing with others made it clear to every inch of my body that I no longer had to be afraid.

In this agricultural school, together with other youth who had been damaged by the Holocaust, I once again learned how to like myself and those around me. I learned to say, "I love you" in ten different languages. I learned to milk cows. And I enjoyed being able to simply walk down the street with my friends. When I wanted to, I picked an orange from the trees and ate it on the spot.

In 1952, we were drafted into the army, where Miriam trained to become a nurse and got her state certification. I became a technical draftswoman.

I was stationed in Tel Aviv and worked for the Israeli Army for eight years. At this time, I was in love with a boy. And he was in love with me. So I was to meet his parents. His mother told me beforehand in confidence that "if you have gotten the idea in your head to marry my son, I'll make your life a living hell."

Thanks a lot, I thought to myself.

Incidentally, the reason she had rejected me was that I had no family to speak of. That was so incomprehensible to me that I said to her, "I don't want to speak with you anymore. How can you say that it's my fault I have no parents?!"

It would have made no sense to marry into a family that disapproved of me through and through. Never again would I be unwanted or disapproved of the way I had experienced for more than half my life so far.

However, her objection reminded me of a fact I had managed to successfully repress—I had no family. That was the Nazis' doing. But it shouldn't go so far as to stop me from starting my own family.

That's why I was so glad to meet an American tourist in April 1960. His name was Michael Kor, and he was visiting his brother in Tel Aviv. Although we could barely communicate with each other, we got married two weeks later.

Michael, nicknamed Mickey, had also been a prisoner in the camps.

The Kor family had lived in Riga, the capital of Latvia. There were four sons, Mickey was the youngest. Father Sholom was a shoemaker and simply didn't have enough money to bring his family to safety from the Nazis. On July 1, 1941, German troops seized the city and all of the Jews were forced to go into the "Moscow suburb," a neighborhood in southern Riga where Russians and Jews traditionally lived. On October 25, the ghetto was sealed off and on that day Sholom was killed. Mickey's mother, Mirka, had to fight to survive alone with four sons in the ghetto.

In December, the SS soldiers selected youth from the ghetto to be forced laborers. Although Mickey was just thirteen years old, he looked older and strong, so his mother pushed him into the row of youth who were able to work. That's how Mickey survived the fate of his mother, who was killed together with 27,500 Latvian and German Jews in the forest of Rumbula.

In April 1945, Michael fled during a death march from a satellite camp of Buchenwald. As the Allied troops arrived, he came out of hiding and joined the soldiers of the American Army. They were led by a lieutenant colonel from Terre Haute,

Indiana. The moment a soldier handed Mickey a bottle of Coca Cola, he knew he was free.

The battalion treated Mickey like he was one of them and even sewed him a GI jacket. Mickey spoke multiple languages, so they soon made use of him as a translator. And he became friends with the lieutenant colonel, a man named Andrew Nehf, who offered the boy his help. After the war, Mickey accepted his offer and immigrated to Terre Haute, a small town about an hour southwest of Indianapolis.

Lieutenant Nehf organized a foster family for Mickey, where he could live the first few years. Mickey completed his high school diploma, studied pharmacy, and became a pharmacist in Terre Haute. He maintained close contact with his rescuer. Nehf, a civil engineer and enthusiastic hobby pianist in his everyday life, taught Mickey to play the piano. Later, he was like a grandfather to our children, Alex and Rina. He was the grandfather they never had, and a friend and counselor to me up until his death in 1984.

In Israel, when I asked Mickey why, of all places in the world, he chose Terre Haute, Indiana, to settle in, he said, "I thought that a town where good people like Lieutenant Nehf come from couldn't be a bad place."

Before I knew what was happening, I was a married woman and lived in the midwestern US—with two suitcases this time. That was all.

I did not speak a word of English. And being Jewish wasn't exactly taken for granted.

In retrospect, you could say that moving from Tel Aviv to Terre Haute was similar to landing on the moon.

It was far, far away.

It was far away from my sister. But also far away from Auschwitz.

Dr. Mengele and his accomplices, the torture and murder; all of that disappeared—suppressed, displaced, recessed into somewhere else. Even Mickey didn't mention the subject. It was almost as if it had never happened. What a model victim I was. No hard feelings!

I imagined that I was doing well with this approach. For when the ghosts of the past knocked at my door, they only weighed me down. What remained was hate.

And hate gnaws at you, hate destroys. The main victim of hate is the person harboring this hate. I really was a model victim.

3

How I Was Able to Forgive

So I lived on the moon, and felt more uneasy from day-to-day. But what should I do instead? Return to Israel? It would have made sense, also because of my deep connection to my twin sister, who lived there. In addition, I had always felt extremely responsible for her, almost the way a mother feels about her children. Particularly ever since Auschwitz. But this feeling of responsibility also had a dark side that would show itself later.

Of all times, during the aftermath of the Summer of Love, in the summer of 1969, when I had finally returned to visit Israel and was seriously considering moving back, Miriam developed full-blown tuberculosis.

It was the second stage in which lung tuberculosis spreads to all of the bones via the bloodstream. It is a rare form of the disease that often eludes diagnosis. Due to her kidney problems, Miriam's immune system was at an all-time low. She had been in the hospital for three months—which I wasn't aware of! As was no one in her closer circle of family and friends; not even her children knew. Only her husband and doctor were privy to her illness.

Miriam had intentionally kept her illness secret because she didn't want her children to be ostracized. If her tuberculosis diagnosis had become common knowledge, it would have certainly led to panicked reactions in the school and the neighborhood. Their children's friends would have been warned against playing with Miriam's children. The fears of infection would have likely lasted for months.

I know about this because I also carry a memento of Dr. Mengele inside me. My own tuberculosis remained undiscovered for many years. Even when I had to be X-rayed before I enrolled in the Israeli Army. At the time, the doctor told me, "You have something in your left lung that worries us. We cannot accept you before we are certain you are healthy."

However, back then I was very thin. One of the precautions was that I should gain five kilos, which was a lot back then. Subsequently, they would test whether the fat covered the questionable spot and whether it would be obscured on the new X-ray. I managed to gain weight and the questionable spot was indeed covered. That's how I was recruited into the Israeli Army, and this *something* in my lung remained undetected.

So for several more years, I was unaware that I had tuberculosis. Although it would accompany me for the rest of my life. And it continues to cause me problems today.

The only thing I knew was that I had a cold virtually nonstop. Just like Miriam did. But we assumed that we were having allergic reactions to different substances. I was tested again and again for different allergies, but no doctor could find anything. To jump ahead: today I hardly get colds anymore. So were they able to find the cause of the allergies?

No—but I want to delve further into this medical search because it explains the roundabout way by which I learned about my legacy from Auschwitz.

✻ ✻ ✻

When I turned sixty-one—around fifty years after my torture—I developed a severe sore throat that didn't improve after four months. I obediently swallowed different antibiotics for more than sixteen weeks, but nothing changed. I came home from giving a talk at a nearby school and told my husband, "I will make some dinner and then please drive me to the hospital. Something isn't right. Every time I breathe, my heart hurts. And my sore throat isn't improving."

The doctor in the hospital ran several tests and said, "You have pericardial inflammation." He explained to me that the pericardium surrounds the entire heart and prevents the heart chambers from becoming distended or excessively dilated. In addition, it is double-walled. That means that it has an outer part (parietal pericardium) and an inner part (epicardium) that is connected to the heart muscle. The space between the inner and outer part is filled with a small amount of liquid in order to help the walls to glide more easily as the heart pumps. If the pericardium becomes inflamed, then it causes intense chest pain, particularly when you breathe.

This pain is caused by the inflamed walls of the pericardium rubbing against each other. Moreover, a pericardial effusion can also arise—when too much liquid builds up in the tissue between the two layers of the pericardium—as it did in my case. This liquid also collected in my lungs. When I breathed, the pericardium pressed against my heart. This type of infection is very rare.

My son worked at a clinic in Cleveland at the time, and he said to me, "Mom, the best specialists work here; you should come."

An older doctor examined me and said, "Okay, Eva, I need the entire medical history of your family."

I answered, "Doctor, you will be glad, because it's very short. It all ended at Auschwitz."

"Oh, you are a survivor?"

"Yes," I answered quietly.

"Then I know what is wrong with you," the doctor said. "You had tuberculosis when you were in Auschwitz. And when you have this disease once, the bacteria remains in your body for the rest of your life. When you become older or weaker, due to other health issues, then the tuberculosis bacteria multiply very quickly and attack other organs. In your case, your heart."

"But I didn't have tuberculosis in the camp," I answered.

That meant my illness remained a mystery for the time being.

However, Miriam had the same problems. At some point we were able to deduct that we had not simply *caught* tuberculosis in Auschwitz.

No, Mengele's doctors must have intentionally injected us with the tuberculosis bacteria. And as the illness progressed— or the first signs were evident in the blood test—then they injected us with additional medications to prevent the illness from fully developing. Thus the bacteria remained in our bodies without our knowledge, and Mengele's accomplices didn't fight the bacteria, but simply held them in check. It was precisely measured so that the tuberculosis could never fully break out, nor could we become aware of it.

Since I learned that, I have to take a variety of different medications, as well as garlic and zinc, and I am constantly cold. Yes, I am very sensitive to the cold.

⚹ ⚹ ⚹

But to come back to Miriam: In late 1969, I returned to Israel, away from the "moon," in order to see if I could find a job there and maybe even an apartment. I met up with sick Miriam—without knowing the cause of it—and saw a woman without any energy, without determination. And, once again, I wanted to get involved with all my strength.

The house in which I visited her seemed neglected. Instead of looking for a job, first I moved into her house. I thought, *I have to take care of Miriam now.* Just like I did before.

If I had known what was really going on at the time, I wouldn't have hesitated for a moment; but, instead I contemplated that if I really went back to Israel, then I would be doing *exactly that* for the rest of my life. And that wouldn't have been good for Miriam or for me. I felt too close to her, and I would be constantly involved in her life.

No matter how I judged the condition of her house, the most important thing was for Miriam to take charge of her life. It wouldn't be helpful if I constantly gave her the feeling that she couldn't manage without me. I didn't give her enough recognition as it was. And at the same time, I couldn't be the one always charging around the corner to her rescue.

It was better to live in another corner of the world and to meet up for special occasions. I had to let her live her own life. But our special connection remained unaffected.

On the other hand, it would have been impossible for Miriam and her family to move to America. With all of her illnesses, without health insurance in America, I would have had to provide her complete financial support. That would have exceeded my capabilities by far.

So I flew back to the moon by myself. But for good this time.

Back to America.

Where I sat in front of the television for hours to escape my loneliness. Alone in this other world.

Once I saw a movie about a young couple in love. The couple caressed each other with words that I didn't understand, but which I immediately wrote down so I could look them up in my dictionary. Finally, I memorized these words. With this method, I learned to speak English well enough to communicate within three months.

And now I wanted to work.

My husband said, "Who, do you think, would employ a woman with two children at home?"

I replied, "Then we'll look for a nanny."

Despite all the hurdles, at the time I was convinced that there had to be a solution to every problem. And despite all the sadness, I was full of hope that my new home would also gladly accept me at some point.

Initially, I worked in a boutique and sold clothes, while I also worked as an English teacher for immigrants. Then I hired myself out as a real estate agent and earned two thousand dollars—

annually. It was actually absurd, but I didn't want to quit my job because that would mean I had failed. I knew I would be able to close more sales when I finally got a real chance. Some people didn't want to give me a chance, though, because I had a fairly pronounced, fairly hard accent. When I heard that for the first time, I was insulted. I survived Auschwitz, and these people think I can't sell houses? Just because of my accent?!

In this sense, I would always live alongside others as a foreign element and, even after thirty years, still be pigeonholed in the role of the foreigner. That was not exactly pleasant.

Although Terre Haute is a university town, the city is anything but cosmopolitan. Out of the 6,000 residents, around 85 percent of them are white, with Anglo-Saxon background. Since tourists rarely end up visiting Terre Haute and businesspeople from abroad don't have much to do there, few people there ever have much contact with foreigners. That leads to aloofness and mistrust when they do meet foreigners. Likewise, trust is the most important quality in the real estate business. Customers have to be able to trust you; otherwise, you'll never get a foot in the door.

I was at odds with everything. And I was full of resentment— of course against the Nazis, who were responsible for it all. But also against myself because I couldn't manage to free myself from these feelings.

At the time I wrote a poem to somehow express how unjustly treated I felt I had been. I have kept these verses to myself until now, but since they depict my feelings at the time so well, I don't want to keep them to myself any longer:

ABC from Auschwitz

A is for Auschwitz—a place close to hell,

B is for Birkenau—where brave children dwell,

C is for Children—standing Czell Apell

D is for Dead people—bodies everywhere,

E is for Experiments—done on me in labs,

F is for the Food—I so seldom had,

G is for Gas chambers—where people had no chance,

H is for High Voltage—in the huge barbed-wire fence,

I is for the Ink—that was burned into my flesh,

J is for Justice—that was sold out for cash,

K is for Kapo—a monster with a whip,

L is for the Lice—that seemed to creep and creep,

M is for Dr. Mengele—The Angel of Death foreman,

N is for Nazis—seemed devils, not human,

O is for the Orphan—I very young became,

P is Potatoes—I organized (stole) at aim,

Q is for the Queasy—that my stomach cried in vain,

R is for the Rats—that my bread were often stealing,

S is for the human-Soap—I washed with without knowing,

T is for the Tattoo—that my arm will always bear,

U is for the Universe—that didn't seem to care,

V is for the Victory—that finally arrived,

W is for the World—that left me so deprived,

X is for the X-rays—that my body often had,

Y is for the Years—of pain in childhood I had,

Z is for the Zest—of life that makes me glad not mad.

The last verse already indicates that I was ready to fight—for my life, for my peace, for my right to happiness. After all, I had tackled the biggest problem that a person could ever have, and I had escaped hell. I would also get a handle on the few problems that I had now. I *willed* it.

≯ ⋆ ≯

In my job, I decided that I would no longer address the prejudices against me, but from now on work as much as humanly possible. I went from door to door—the hard school of cold sales—and rang at every door, asking people if they perhaps wanted to sell their house.

That type of work is very hard-going. You have to give up all of your pride. But even though this step was necessary, I told myself that I would still do it. It took me six years until I could distribute business cards in mailboxes with ease.

Back then I worked for a small real estate agency, with no outlook of getting a satisfying income. However, twice a year I visited people in the major real estate offices to put in a good word for myself. Word had gotten around about my approach. "Is it true," the CEO asked me, "that you do the hard-slogging tour, going door-to-door?"

"Yes."

"Then I want you!"

I got a job at the biggest real estate company in the entire county. They weren't really convinced that I could make sales because I still had this same, pronounced accent and, moreover, there were top sellers who were selling multimillion-dollar real estate—but they wanted to try their luck with me. I was in competition with at least thirty of these turbo-sellers. Per house, my earnings were modest, so I was determined to sell even more of the little houses. And that turned into quite a large number. So many that I was allowed to stay on.

At some point I even decided to use my accent as a unique selling point. I will turn my obstacle into an advantage. So I had a new business card made, which read: *Eva Kor Mozes—the woman with the accent.*

After all, I cannot change who I am.

I associate the good times in these early years with my kids. My son Alex was born in 1961, my daughter Rina in 1963. I was a good mother, a loving mother, but at some point my two kids asked me, "Mom, why don't we have any grandparents?"

"There were some mean people in the world," I replied. "People called them Nazis ...They killed your grandparents ..."

That was enough in the beginning. They were still too little for all the rest. But I knew that there would be more questions with time, and even though I was horrified at this prospect, I didn't want to lie to my children the way my parents had. I had asked Mother and Father about Hitler, again and again; I had bombarded them with rumors. And they always answered, "We will protect you." And besides, Hitler was far away. And the Nazis would never come to our little village.

But they came!

My parents should have said, "We will do everything in our power, but we cannot promise you that the Nazis won't come here one day."

That would have been honest.

Over the years, I associated thoughts of my parents not only with the pain of losing them but with bitterness at them having lied to me.

Today, of course, I understand that that was terribly unfair and egotistical of me. And it only came from the hate inside me—not only toward the Nazis but toward the whole world that was conspiring against me and, of all people, how unfair that I experienced so much misfortune. My parents were truly convinced that Hitler would never come to our little village in the countryside, to snatch six insignificant, innocent Jews. So they stayed in their village.

You could call them naive, but you could also say that they were optimists. And they were the type of people who believed nothing bad could happen to them—that those things only happened to other people.

That is a good attitude, and I'm glad I inherited it, too. What kind of life would it be if you woke up every day fearful about everything that might happen to you?

No, we go to work in the morning, and we want to have a good day. When things take a different turn, and aren't as good as we hoped, then we still accept it, but we don't abandon our good faith.

I wanted to spare my children the experience of feeling like an outsider. But there were confusing situations again and again. For instance, there was this big holiday in December that Americans in particular make such a big deal about. It's called Christmas. What were we supposed to do as a Jewish family?

My daughter Rina was four years old and went to preschool, where the kids made beautiful Christmas decorations. She came home and proudly announced, "Mom, we have to hang it up!"

And I told her, "No!"

And Rina whined, "But Mom, we made it all by ourselves."

"No."

On the other hand, I couldn't flat-out reject her. So I had to find a solution. I suddenly had an idea. I drove to a piano store and asked, "Do you have an empty box? One you would normally transport a piano?"

We placed the box in an empty room, and this arrangement was declared their personal playroom. They could decorate it as they saw fit, and they could also hang up their Christmas decorations inside. In the end, this box became so popular that the kids played with it for five whole years, and their friends even came to our house just to play in the box. They crafted their own windows and curtains inside and they turned it into a true kid's playhouse, complete with furniture and dishes.

However, I felt helpless when it came to another holiday: Halloween.

My son Alex was six years old and, of course, he was captivated by all the costumes and pranks. He had no idea that the pranks reminded me of the times we were bullied by the Nazi youth in Portz—a time in which I was helpless and could do nothing to defend myself.

So I didn't join in the celebrations; on the contrary, I shooed the children away.

Word got around, which just made things worse. From then on, the harassment began every year on October 31. The children painted swastikas on the house, and they wrote "Go home, you dirty Jews." They even placed white crosses on the lawn. It was awful. And I reacted very emotionally. I was hurt in a way that these people couldn't understand. Every year on October 31, images from the past came back to haunt me—and I didn't want to see these images or these children.

Of course Halloween is mainly about shocking one's fellow human beings. And they knew how to shake me to the core. Moreover, they had the support of their parents, which bothered me even more. No one could understand me. Instead, I continued to only shoo away the children.

Alex came home from school crying and said, "Mom, I am so embarrassed because of you! Everyone says you're crazy."

"You can have fun with your friends," I answered. "But you cannot go to strangers' houses and do that kind of thing. Besides, there is a reason that I am different than the other mothers."

These Halloween tricks had started when Alex was six, and now he was in puberty. It seemed as if it would never end, it had already become a ritual—driving the crazy lady up the wall. Alex had to listen to everyone saying how crazy his mother was, and how you could have great fun at her expense.

The youth threw dry kernels of corn at our windows, which sounded like machine guns firing to me.

So I wrote a letter to the editor of our local newspaper. I politely asked everyone to stop pulling pranks. "I am happy to give out sweets," I wrote, "but I cannot handle the pranks. It catapults me back to a dark time when I was helpless." But no one wanted to understand me.

"They say you are a crazy survivor," Alex told me.

I defended myself, saying, "I am not crazy. But it's true, I am a survivor."

It is an extremely hard situation to try to explain something to your son without completely understanding what's going on in your own mind.

"Mom, why can't you be like the other mothers?"

"I am not crazy," I answered, "but I am definitely not like the other mothers."

✶ ✶ ✶

I had already considered telling my story to people in order to explain to all these neighbors why I reacted so sensitively, but I just didn't know how to go about it.

I had been bullied for eleven years up until 1978, when NBC aired the series *Holocaust* and school children were confronted with the film.

All of a sudden, everyone understood why I was different. I was even approached in the supermarket, people called me. Suddenly, people apologized, "We had no idea . . ."

On the other hand, when this TV series was broadcasted, it flooded me with memories that I had suppressed until then. And then there was no stopping them. More and more details surfaced.

Now I unpacked my box of family photos—for the first time since I had moved to Terre Haute. I had completely suppressed all of these memories, blocked them out, and pushed them into the furthest corner of my mind. Now the memories were coming back to me. Auschwitz was back.

I decided to face Auschwitz. And I failed immediately. How to fathom the unfathomable, how to say the unsayable? And besides—what did I know anyway?

People were constantly asking about the particulars—about the camp itself, the gas chambers, the type of experiments that Dr. Mengele carried out. But I had never found out the details about them. I was at one of the selections, and I knew the girls' camp, the infirmary, the laboratory. And I had seen and experienced terrible things there. But how it had all worked and the purpose behind my torture? All of that was a mystery to me.

I thought there must be tons of information available about the camps and about Dr. Mengele and his atrocities. And I began to investigate myself. But oddly enough, I could find no leads about the nature of his research or results of any kind.

Instead, all kinds of experts were making claims; experts who supposedly knew everything about us victims.

These experts ceaselessly claimed we felt guilty because we survived, and that we victims were ashamed of our experiences and that's why we talked so little about our experiences.

Of course that was nonsense. I was always proud that I survived. I have never felt guilty about surviving. I couldn't talk about my experiences for several years because I didn't have the capacity to replenish the emotional energy it would cost me. In a sense, I was a starving soul.

In the meantime, I was no longer afraid of my memories, but there are still many suppressed memories. However, my traumatic past doesn't paralyze me, and it no longer prevents me from being the person I want to be.

I gave lots of presentations—between 1978 and 1985, it must have been over 100—and I was always cool, calm, and collected. I didn't think I was still filled with hate. It was my attitude at the time. I woke up in the morning, took care of my two kids, went to work, and somehow struggled along. As an outsider, as a real estate agent with a scorned accent. I gave my presentations, but I spoke very superficially about something that seemingly didn't have much to do with me. And I always ended my talks with the admission, "I know that all of these things happened to me, but I always feel like I'm standing next to my former self, this little girl who is telling her story."

No one ever asked about the end of my presentation.

After the *Holocaust* series, it took me another six years before I had the idea to create an organization to help me and Miriam find other "Mengele twins." In 1984, we founded the organization CANDLES, which stands for Children of Auschwitz Nazi Deadly Lab Experiments Survivors. We were able to find 122 survivors. Until today, we strive to uncover the medical consequences and background of the experiments since many survivors cannot be treated correctly without this information.

I know how frustrated I was back then since so few Nazis had been convicted in Germany. They were walking around freely. *The Germans were in cahoots with the Nazis* is what I thought back then. When a grandchild discovered that there was a former Nazi in the family, he or she was not obligated to get in touch with the public prosecutor's office. On the contrary, the Germans stick together and protect their own (or so I thought). They live with these criminals as their next door neighbors, seemingly as a matter of course. But silently.

That was also the year when I returned to Auschwitz for the first time after liberation. Furthermore, I was on my own.

Back then, Poland was one of the satellite countries of the Soviet Union. And Auschwitz was in Poland. It was incredibly hard to communicate with Auschwitz; there was no internet back then, just faxing or possibly a phone call. It took months for me to receive a reply.

But I had decided to visit the camp. The best connection for me was with Lufthansa airline, via Vienna.

I hadn't given this much thought, but in the plane, I was suddenly surrounded by German voices—for the first time in decades. They were everywhere—German jokes, German laughter, German whispering—and all of that suddenly transported me back to the selection ramp. It was 1984, but I was trapped back in 1944!

My stomach was queasy. We were already in the air, and I could no longer stop the plane.

Upon my arrival in Vienna, I felt physically ill and was in a terrible mental state. My original idea was to take a tour through Vienna's Old Town and then continue on to Katowice on a train. But I had become paranoid.

I covered my camp tattoo and was in fact convinced that every person over sixty would immediately jump on me and beat me up. It was crazy!

I covered up my tattoo for the first time in my life. I had never done that before and have never done it since.

If I had taken another airline, any other airline, everything would have been fine. But this Deutsch, Deutsch, Deutsch reminded me of *"Raus! Raus! Raus!"* It was the first time since Auschwitz that I heard these sounds in my immediate surroundings.

A tour of the city was out of the question. Instead, I went to the train station immediately and luckily met a young Polish woman there who had lived in Italy and wanted to travel to Katowice with her mother. She spoke English and helped me to translate. I was panicked. I feared for my life! On a rational level, of course I understood that the world had changed since 1945, but apparently my body didn't feel this way and was stuck in the past.

In the meantime, it was the middle of the night. All around me there was complete darkness.

The train crossed through a little corner of Czechoslovakia, which you needed a visa for in those days. The woman in the American travel agency hadn't known about that. And all of a sudden police officers in uniform were checking the train. They looked very unfriendly and asked for my visa.

I had no idea what was going on, and I had no idea about Czechoslovakia since I was going to Poland, to Auschwitz.

Along the train tracks, a light went on and I could see a little police station there.

"Come with me!" The stranger demanded. I told the Polish woman, "Please ask him which papers I should sign and how much a visa costs. But here in the train!" The travel agency had made a mistake, but there was nothing in the world that could convince me to leave this train and follow someone into that remotely located building in the middle of the night. Never!

So I paid around $150.00 and got the visa.

When I arrived in Katowice, I was exhausted.

Back then, it was the most desolate, dark, and depressing place I had ever seen in the world since I had left Auschwitz. And no one spoke English. The only foreign language people spoke was Russian. I was back in Communism.

It was very early in the morning. I still managed to find a hotel, without a porter, with cold water, with five-bed rooms and a toilet in the hall. Drunk people were already walking the streets.

I wasn't deterred by that and looked for a taxi that would take me to Auschwitz.

When I arrived, I fortunately found two people with whom I had corresponded, at least by name. I was so exhausted from my travels that I didn't exchange much small talk, and cut to the chase. I asked one of the women, "Is there a place here known as Birkenau?"

She was a little surprised. "Of course there is."

You have to know that a professor who had visited Auschwitz before me came back telling everyone that Auschwitz was all that was left; Birkenau had been burned down. And that made me furious.

"I have to see it. Right away."

And then I saw the big entrance building, the railroad tracks— it was all there, again! Covered by grass and soil. We walked through it. All the way to the monument.

In the memories of my childhood, Auschwitz was enormous. I remember huge buildings that towered over my head like dark clouds. Now I had to figure out for myself: does Auschwitz really exist the way I remember it? Or was it the product of my imagination?

I asked the woman from the museum, "Where is the selection ramp?"

She looked at me as if I was not quite all there. "Ms. Kor, you have been walking around on it the whole time."

"That cannot be so," I replied.

"It is."

The next day, I came back alone with a cassette recorder to record my thoughts. I was disturbed, something wasn't right. Where was the ramp? I walked around, looked all around me, until I saw a tiny little piece of cement that hadn't been covered in grass. *That* was the selection ramp.

The way I remember it, all of this had been concrete—new, bright, completely covered in concrete—but in the present, I was walking on grass.

No one had taken care of the complex, so weeds and grass had taken over.

I took a photo of this narrow strip of concrete. In comparison to the memories of my childhood, for the first time I became aware that the ramp reached all the way into the camp. It was done at the suggestion of Rudolf Höss, as I knew, so he could more effectively eliminate the Hungarian arrivals.

I closed my eyes and abandoned myself to the moment. Everything came back to me. I heard sounds, voices, stronger than faded photographs.

Voices can be more frightening than other memories. And I thought about my paranoid fit in Austria, when I had been so jarred by the casual chatter of passers-by. *I don't want that anymore,* I thought. *I want to live my life without complicated trapdoors inside of me. I do not want to live in fear any longer.*

⋆ ⋆ ⋆

In 1991, I traveled to Berlin with my sister to participate in a documentary about different Holocaust survivors. We visited the Berlin Wall, and one of the first things I did was to buy a dictionary. German is a wonderful language, and it would never make me afraid again, I decided; so I dedicated myself to the language and intentionally eavesdropped.

Don't run away from it, but run toward it! I have managed well with this approach ever since.

This attitude toward life also chipped away my inner protection wall slowly but surely. I can still clearly remember the day I gave a talk at Indiana State University in 1985. I described the separation from my mother in Auschwitz, and I suddenly began to sob. Then I started to cry uncontrollably—for the first time since liberation. I was confused and embarrassed since I didn't normally carry a handkerchief with me. I had never needed one. After all, I had always kept a cool head— but now I was crying uncontrollably. I cried because I could once again feel all of the pain, all the fear and horror I had experienced in Auschwitz. From then on I never again ended another presentation by saying that I was telling the story of a little girl.

That evening, the little girl and I became one. I suddenly found the child I thought I had lost in Auschwitz.

But my life once again spiraled out of control in another area. In 1987, my son was diagnosed with testicular cancer. They predicted less than a 50 percent chance of survival. He had chemotherapy and lost his hair. For two weeks, I cried and cried. Why me, why me?!

At the time I was fifty-three years old, Alex was twenty-six. And in the same year, Miriam became ill again. Yet again!

Over the years, Miriam had had increasingly serious problems with her kidneys. We knew that it had to do with the injections they had given her in Auschwitz. These problems had already become apparent during her first pregnancy in 1960. Miriam's body no longer responded to antibiotics. In 1963, during her second pregnancy, it became even worse. This intolerance to medications was so uncommon that the doctors devoted themselves to searching for the cause and discovered that her kidneys had stopped developing at the stage of a ten-year-old child's kidneys.

After the birth of her third baby in 1967, her kidneys failed completely. I flew to Israel and donated my left kidney to her. The hospital had already seen thousands of transplants that had been carried out smoothly. But something wasn't right with Miriam. It was another complication that baffled the doctors.

They figured out the medication that was supposed to prevent the body from rejecting the transplanted kidney was being attacked by an indefinable substance in her body. Miriam was spitting up blood. She was in terrible condition. The doctors were certain this mysterious substance had been growing in her body since the Auschwitz experiments and had caused bladder cancer, but they didn't know what to do about it.

Up until now, I have still not been able to figure out the nature of the tests they had carried out on Miriam and me in Auschwitz, and I probably never will. From the few documents that could be found in Auschwitz, they could only determine that my blood had been tested for blood urea nitrogen, sodium chloride, takata-ara (a test for disturbances in protein metabolism), and vitamin C.

In addition, I was tested for syphilis and scarlet fever. Although Mengele's results had been sent to a scientific institute in Berlin, I found no records there.

When Miriam's condition worsened for the last time in 1993, I decided to have her flown to America, to a special clinic dedicated to chemotherapy.

"How high are my chances?" She asked her doctor.

"Two percent" was his answer.

"Two percent is better than zero percent."

If we had been able to find our Auschwitz files and thus finally a clue to the nature of the experiments, Miriam's life could have likely been saved.

After the treatment Miriam returned to Israel, where she died on June 6, 1993, because the cancer had spread to her brain. I found out about her death from a message from Miriam's husband on my answering machine. "We are sorry to inform you that your sister has died."

I had just returned from a property viewing appointment.

An official message, that was all. I wasn't even able to touch her one last time. Miriam, who had always been my second self. Her death completely threw me off track.

And I started having nightmares again.

And I cried for many, many hours on end. Now the Nazis had finally managed to kill Miriam. I was the last survivor of the Kor family from Portz. And I decided to hate the Nazis even more than I had up until then. And to do everything in my power to find out what Dr. Mengele had done to us. Everything!

One month after Miriam's death, I received a call from Boston; it was an invitation to a conference. My motivation was low, but I couldn't wallow in mourning forever, and moreover, I had a vague feeling that it was the right decision to go.

I was supposed to give a presentation at Boston University, and the hosting professor told me it would be nice if an Auschwitz doctor could also come along.

I was standing in the kitchen while we talked on the phone, and I said, "Do you have any idea where I could find such a person? I don't think they advertise in the telephone directory."

The professor replied, "Ms. Kor, I know you like to make jokes, but do consider it."

The idea would not leave me in peace. Not because I longed to stand face-to-face with an actual doctor from Auschwitz—an accomplice of the man who had irreparably damaged me in body and soul, and who had sentenced my sister to a long and painful death. But because perhaps this would finally lead me to records about Miriam and myself and all the other so-called "Mengele twins".

I remembered that in 1991, I had participated in a TV program on Auschwitz produced by a German film team. It had been uncommonly cold, and that's why they served hot chocolate in a Mercedes during the breaks. In addition, all of the team members had constantly greeted each other with kisses. It was a strange atmosphere. At the time, I had received a copy of the film, but had never watched it. Then I put it in the video player, and there was a former doctor from Auschwitz!

His name was Dr. Hans Münch.

He had been accused of being a war criminal, but had been found not guilty after countless Auschwitz survivors spoke out on his behalf. After that, he practiced undisturbed as a doctor in Allgäu.

I had to sit down for a minute.

I contacted the German television team and told them about Miriam's death. She had been involved in the production and I was hoping they would give me the number since I was asking in her memory. I also told them about the conference in Boston. "Please give me Dr. Münch's telephone number."

I received a fax in response—with the private telephone number of a Nazi doctor.

At the time, I was friends with Toni, a former Dutch resistance activist who spoke very good German. He promised me that he would call Dr. Münch and then get in touch with me.

"Eva," he told me on the phone after a few hours had passed, "Dr. Münch is not coming to Boston, but he is willing to meet you at his home in Germany."

Wow, I thought, and had to sit down again. What should I do now? I didn't understand why this man wanted to see me. If I am honest, I still don't understand it today. But meeting in Germany, in his house, had been his idea. He had turned down other survivors who had requested to meet him.

I don't know what has to happen so that things come together in our lives. I do not want to speculate about whether there are higher powers, angels, or anything else like that. The fact remains that I cannot explain certain strokes of fortune that have happened in my life.

⁎ ⁎ ⁎

So in 1993, I traveled to Germany and met a Nazi doctor in Roßhaupten. And nothing happened the way I had previously imagined. He didn't make excuses for himself in a detached, cool way. Instead, he admitted to and repented for his actions. And I didn't descend into feelings of hatred. Instead, I realized that I liked him.

He hadn't been as bad as the other Nazis, he once told me casually. I wouldn't necessarily agree. He was a henchman of death, an accomplice of Dr. Mengele, and his workplace was somewhere that served no other purpose than to kill people— hundreds of thousands of them. And he knew this. He was aware of it all the time. That's what had deprived him of sleep for the last fifty years.

The admission that I liked him shocked me more than the knowledge that he couldn't help me with my main reason for coming. Dr. Münch had no idea about the nature or even the results of Mengele's human experiments, let alone about the documents.

But he had lots of information about the gas chambers, and that's how I heard about the way my parents and sisters had been killed for the first time—presumably from an eyewitness. "The people were told that they were going to shower, they were supposed to remember the number of their clothes hook and tie their shoes together."

He said that they even sprayed perfume in order to make it very realistic.

"When the gas chambers were completely full, the doors were hermetically sealed and made airtight. In the ceiling, a vent was opened that was reminiscent of an air vent, and a pebble-like granulate was poured through the opening. This granulate worked like dry ice, and turned into a gas. The gas began to rise from the ground.

"The people tried to escape the rising gas and climbed on top of each other. The strongest reached the top of the mountain of entangled bodies. The moment the people at the top of the pile had stopped moving—I looked through the peephole and watched everything—then I knew that everyone was dead."

Dr. Münch had insisted that he hadn't been involved in the selections, and they had believed him. He didn't want to be responsible for who would live and who would die, he said. That would be playing God, and he didn't want to do that.

I personally consider it to be impossible that an employee in Auschwitz could act independently and remain morally upright. I told him so, too. However, I also told him that I no longer wanted to blame him. *Pardon me?*

While I was sitting with him in his living room, I writhed inside at my spontaneous comment. *What had I just said?* I remembered all of the cowardly answers of the former Nazis; they said they had never wanted everything to happen. It was all Hitler's fault. Or Mengele's. They had only carried out orders. And the other Nazis had been much worse.

Should I meticulously consider the details of their statements? In order to then judge which Nazis were worse than the others? That is a punishment for me as a victim!

And I no longer wanted to punish myself.

I still wasn't ready to truly understand this new path I was on, but I could definitely sense that I couldn't actually forgive Dr. Münch, the supposedly "good" Nazi, but not forgive the others, but perhaps forgive some of them after comparing and judging their crimes. I didn't want to deal with all the painful details.

In this moment, in the living room of Dr. Hans Münch, it was important to me that he admitted to signing the mass death certificates—an extremely significant piece of information for posterity.

Subsequently, I asked him if he wanted to go to Auschwitz with me in 1995, when we celebrated the fiftieth anniversary of our liberation from the camp. I also asked him to sign a sworn declaration of everything he had seen and done and to do so at the site of all the murders. Without hesitation, he agreed.

At that moment I was so thankful that I wanted to show him my appreciation.

I still consider this document to be very, very important since there are still neo-Nazis and revisionists running around and saying that there were no concentration camps, that no one was gassed, that it wasn't technically possible—but Dr. Münch, who had seen it all with his own eyes in Auschwitz, said without a moment's hesitation, "I would be glad to sign such a document."

I have never analyzed his behavior. Whether it was an attempt to find forgiveness or repentance, I have no idea. But upon returning to Terre Haute, I felt compelled to thank him.

It was clear to me that most people wouldn't think of doing such a thing—of thanking a Nazi for something. As I talked with my friends and family members about it, everyone discouraged me from my plan. But I wouldn't let myself be swayed. I was determined but also completely on my own with my idea. And I didn't know where to find an appropriate gift. What form could such a gift take?

So I drove to a gift shop, looked around the greeting card section, and as was to be expected, I found nothing. Not even when I consulted a saleswoman. I drove back home, without a gift and without any ideas.

However, never give up! That is my famous motto in life.

While I was cooking, vacuuming, washing up, driving, I was constantly brainstorming: what could I possibly give to Dr. Münch as a token of appreciation?

I was constantly racking my brain, when after ten long months I suddenly had a simple revelation: *What about a letter in which I forgive him for everything?*

I knew immediately that Dr. Münch would greatly appreciate a letter like that, but I also discovered something else—namely, what power I actually possessed. I had the power to forgive!

And no one could give me this power, no one could take it away. It was solely in my control and I could use it however I saw fit.

An amazing discovery.

Up to this point in time, I had simply reacted to everything that people had done to me. I had acted just like victims tend to act. They do not feel like they have control over their lives. So, instead, they react to what other people say and do.

Now it suddenly dawned on me: I am in control of my life. *I have power.*

That was fascinating.

So I began to write the letter. I had no idea how I should proceed, there was no formula for writing a letter of forgiveness to a Nazi; it took me another four months.

After I finished the letter, I thought my written English might not be good enough, so I asked my former English teacher to meet me. "I need you to correct a letter for me."

We met up three times, and after the last meeting, she told me, "Eva, your problem doesn't have to do with Dr. Münch, your true problem is Dr. Mengele. . . ."

At first, I was shocked. Somehow it was clear to me that she was right, but it was overwhelming for me.

She said, "Eva, when you get home, do me a favor. Talk with Dr. Mengele and tell him that you forgive him. And then see how you feel . . ."

I thought it was an interesting idea.

After that, I drove home, closed my door, pulled down a dictionary and wrote a list of insults and curse words. "And despite everything you have done to me," I whispered, "you need to know that I forgive you . . ."

The idea that I could somehow gain the upper hand over Josef Mengele was an incredible experience for me. I was no longer the victim, passive and helpless, but the active person. That made me feel powerful. I realized that forgiveness was freeing—not for the offender, but for the victim.

I didn't need to get revenge, retaliation, or atonement in order to experience this sublime feeling—and I had never thought highly of the Old Testament approach of "an eye for an eye."

I would forgive Dr. Mengele and finally be free. That was my personal epiphany. Free to discover that I had the power over my own today and tomorrow, again and again. It hurt no one, it doesn't hurt me.

And it is free. Everyone can accomplish it.

Also, there are no side effects. It works.

But if you do not like feeling like a free person, it is possible to return to your pain and hatred anytime.

4

What Forgiveness Means to Me

If I can forgive Josef Mengele, I thought, *I can forgive anyone.*

And in these high spirits, I entered Auschwitz on January 27, 1995, to meet Dr. Münch. It was a cold, gray winter's day. In a low pressure area without snow. Dr. Münch, already waiting with his blue coat and hat, hooked his arm under mine and slowly walked with me to the selection ramp. We didn't say a word. When we reached the ramp, he lit a candle and signed the document—testifying that there, where he stood, the decision about who would live and who would die was made arbitrarily; that thousands of people were sent to the gas chambers, were subjected to the pesticide Zyklon B, declared dead "after three to five minutes," and then "removed and burned." That he, Dr. Hans Münch, had to live with this nightmare for fifty years and that he was sorry to have been a part of it.

I thought about all the people whose deaths I witnessed. And then I read my own personal declaration of forgiveness.

Declaration of Amnesty

Auschwitz Fifty Years Later

I, Eva Mozes Kor, a twin who as a child survived Josef Mengele's experiments at Auschwitz fifty years ago, hereby give amnesty to all Nazis who participated directly or indirectly in the murder of my family and millions of others.

I extend this amnesty to all governments who protected Nazi criminals for fifty years, then covered up their acts, and covered up their cover-up.

Fifty years after liberation from Auschwitz, I, Eva Mozes Kor, in my name only, give this amnesty because it is time to go on; it is time to heal our souls; it is time to forgive, but never forget; it is time to open up all the classified and personal files not only for the sake of history but to alleviate human suffering. I, as a Citizen of the Free World, declare here in Auschwitz, that I have the human right to locate my Auschwitz files so I know what germs and chemicals were injected into my body fifty years ago. I expect the leaders of the world to put politics aside and, for the sake of all humanity, assist us in getting our files. Help us make it possible for every Mengele Guinea Pig, for every survivor, to find their files, their stories, their past.

I, the only living member of a very large family, in their name and mine appeal to the US Congress, to the Israeli Knesset, the German legislators, and others who have the power, to pass laws dismantling all Nazi-related investigative units, such as the US Justice Department and Special Investigations, and open up all Nazi files to survivors and the public.

Look up to the skies here in Auschwitz. The souls of millions of victims are with us—and I am saying, with them as witnesses: "Enough is Enough. Fifty Years is More Than Enough." I am healed inside; therefore it gives me no joy to see any Nazi criminal in jail, nor do I want to see any harm come to Josef Mengele, the Mengele family, or their business corporations. I urge all former Nazis to come forward and testify to the crimes they have committed without any fear of further persecution.

Here in Auschwitz, I hope in some small way to send the world a message of forgiveness, a message of peace, a message of hope, a message of healing.

NO MORE WARS, NO MORE EXPERIMENTS WITHOUT INFORMED CONSENT, NO MORE GAS CHAMBERS, NO MORE BOMBS, NO MORE HATRED, NO MORE KILLING, NO MORE AUSCHWITZES.

At this moment, I felt all the pain that I had carried with me for fifty years lifted from my shoulders. I was no longer a victim of Auschwitz. I was no longer a prisoner of my past. I was free.

Free from Mengele and Auschwitz—from this immensely heavy burden that had weighed me to the ground.

All victims carry this hate, this rage inside of themselves; they feel helpless and weak.

I looked up to the sky. And I said to myself, "If people have souls, then millions of souls are flying over the camp right now. And if the souls of my parents are among them, then this is the right moment to finish my business with the Nazis. And to forgive them."

Silently.

I didn't write anything down or speak my intention aloud into the sky, but I forgave my parents.

Yes, my parents!

Weren't my parents the ones who had proven themselves unable to protect me from my fate in Auschwitz?

Nevertheless.

That's right, they didn't protect me from growing up an orphan. And life as an orphan means that I became a different person after my parents disappeared; on one hand, a merciless existence, alone. And on the other hand, the people surrounding me treated me as someone different from then on. Not necessarily better. And when I walked around with other kids, who of course still had parents, to them I was only "the little poor orphan girl."

I have never felt like I belonged anywhere. Yes, I could live with my aunt, but it wasn't the same as living with a loving mother. She did the best she could, but she was also affected by the death of her son. There was no warmth, no affection, no gifts or kisses—all of the things that a child longs for. And expects.

I have to live with these wounds in my soul for the rest of my life.

Even during my happy years in Israel, there were times that were horrible for me as an orphan; for instance, the vacation season. I lived in a lodging house for soldiers; refrigerators were a rare privilege. On the other hand, during holiday breaks, all of the shops were closed. So I always went to my relatives' houses in order to have something to eat. But I was never part of the family. That's why I strived to make myself useful in any way I could to avoid being seen as a freeloader, and I hated it. Even today I don't like to stay in an apartment with several people for longer periods of time. I'd rather go to a hotel so that I don't owe anyone anything.

That is a remnant of my issues as a child.

When I think about my parents or my two sisters, I have often wondered, *Would they be proud of me if they were still alive? Do they somehow know that I have done good things? And have I done all of this because they raised me well?*

There is a certain satisfaction in doing good and I believe my family would like what I have accomplished. I think they would be proud of me. And I'm sure that if they could be with me today, they would also say so.

That is the only type of coming to terms with the past that I don't consider to be destructive or self-tormenting.

✳ ✳ ✳

What made the first thirty years of my life so painful was that while grappling with the past, I had beaten myself down.

I remember one gathering with other Mengele twins in Israel. One woman said, "I don't remember anything that happened in Auschwitz."

I felt affronted. I told her, "You were seven years old. Can't you remember when your mother sneaked in at night?"

"Oh, yes, I remember . . ." the woman responded.

"Do you remember when the overseer hit your mother on the head?"

"Yes. I remember . . ."

"And do you remember how jealous I was of you?

"Yes," she said softly.

"Why was I jealous?"

"Because I had a mother and you didn't," she replied, stock-still.

"That's right," I said. "And I never had a mother after that. Every whisper between you and your mother reminded me that you had a mother and I didn't. It was very hard for me to cope."

During the first thirty years, I always cried on cue when a child character was separated from her mother in a movie. I remember going to see a blockbuster with my daughter in 1979. Rina was sixteen, wild about movies, and she went out to see them practically nonstop. The film was called *Kramer vs. Kramer*. We left the theater and I tried to make conversation about the picture.

"How did you like the story?" I asked my daughter.

"The movie was outstanding," she replied, "but *you* were terrible."

"What? How come?"

"I've never heard of anyone who cries as much as you. It's embarrassing."

"Do you mean to say you didn't cry?!"

"What should I cry about?" my daughter asked, dumbfounded.

"The little boy who gets separated from his mother!"

"And?"

In that moment, I said to myself, "Okay, thank God she can't understand what it means to be separated from her mother." I write "separated" deliberately; the murder machine at Auschwitz did not provide for the dead to be seen off, buried, mourned. So there was always a glimmer of hope that they might have survived, especially when it came to my two older sisters.

Somehow . . . Maybe . . .

* * *

That hope never abandoned me, not even later.

In 1997—over fifty years after the liberation of Auschwitz—I received word that my sister Aliz had survived. I was filled with consternation. I could hardly think or eat or sleep. For all my hope, I had always been forced to assume that Aliz had been killed shortly after arriving at Auschwitz. But in 1997, an international organization contacted me because the name Aliz Mozes had appeared on a list of Holocaust survivors. I was stunned. For a few weeks, I had hope that I would actually be able to hold her in my arms after all those years. I contemplated where she might be living. I had so much to say to her, was delighted beyond description—until I found out that it was another woman with exactly the same name but from an unrelated family.

So I lost Aliz all over again.

That was a terrible moment.

But the hope that somehow, maybe someone could have actually survived, still remained as strong.

Somehow . . .

Yet I don't want such things to bring me to my knees anymore.

When loved ones die in a genocide, we can learn to talk about it, or at least we can try, but I no longer want to be subjugated by that.

We all have the capacity to remember and to commemorate, but that is not all we are. We are human beings who grow beyond our challenges. That is the only way to explain my resolve. Because whenever I talk about it, it usually still feels like looking down upon something happening elsewhere. And yet I am no longer the victim lying on the floor in Auschwitz. I can see it all, remember it all—and I can even recall the pain. But now, whenever the pain cuts too close, I have gained the ability to withdraw. I do not particularly enjoy the feeling of suffering.

Still, I haven't mutated into a robot, shutting myself off from all humanity. Sometimes the pain creeps back. Specifically, the minute I talk about my mother, it becomes very hard for me to hold back tears. That's one thing the past is good at, creeping pitilessly into the present.

Still, this form of distancing is important for my concept of forgiveness because I can observe the past today in all its detail and even describe it in depth, but it doesn't overwhelm me anymore. For instance, in the last twenty years since I began forgiving, I have made a habit of calling to mind a good joke as soon as my feelings threaten to overwhelm me. Or I fixate on painstakingly clear pronunciation so that my voice is not flooded with tears.

Because I really am not a robot.

And because it hurts as much as ever to talk about certain memories. But when I'm crying and grief-stricken, I can't communicate information with clarity as I would like to. If I am overwhelmed by emotion, I only produce anguish. After all, I don't tell my life story to feel bad or to drag other people down—rather, only by means of my biography can I speak about forgiveness and the possibilities it can open up in others.

I am forever aware of what this concept has made possible in my life. I can publish and talk about my experiences daily or even several times a day; and still, I am not eaten up by it.

This is very important in order not to be a victim.

What happens in a victim's mind?

For a long, long time after the actual tragedy is over, most people affected by it remain just that: a *victim*.

And why do they maintain that status?

For one thing, they have never truly healed from what they've been through. That's why they develop various ailments. For another, they are enraged up to their necks. I want to make this clear one more time: no one has ever volunteered to be a victim. No one ever has raised their hand at a public gathering and said, "Hello, I'd absolutely like to . . ."

Before you know it, you are bullied by someone who puts you in a position of no longer having the slightest control over your daily life. Suddenly, a stranger is dictating what will happen to you from here on out. Whether you'll eat and even whether you'll live or die.

All you have of your own is hope. And that's a lot.

A longing to make it through somehow.

However, those who actually have made it through this situation are left with a legacy of enormous rage. Most people are then overwhelmed by that rage. And dramatically wounded. They no longer function the way that human beings normally act. Their lives are lived on the back burner, constantly struggling, powerless, barely capable of managing everyday problems.

They've been trapped by a victim mentality.

That means that if a thief steals their car—a nice one—a year later, they'll say, "I'm always the chump. This always happens to me. And me alone . . ."

That's victim thinking.

In those moments, you are incapable of remembering a pleasant moment, let alone a successful one. Only the bad things are stored in your memory banks. "Why is it always me? Poor me. They always knock me down . . ."

It's rather unlikely that a habitual thief would steal your car specifically because you were humiliated a year ago. And it's very likely that the two occurrences are completely unrelated. But a typical victim associates them. "Bad things only ever happen to me, but good things always happen to my coworker."

Of course, there's a possibility that a typical victim has other psychological issues unrelated to the crime. And there's even a possibility that some of these problems are actually results of the original crime. But I consider both cases quite rare.

Before that, my way of thinking was that of a victim. For example, I broke my ankle more than twenty-five years ago and, for me, that was a crystal-clear consequence of my past. I described the long period of malnutrition during my childhood, compounded by five terrible years of communism added to the atrocious time in Auschwitz on the brink of starvation—a long, long period of malnutrition altogether—and that's why I broke my ankle in America. An obvious conclusion.

Even though somebody told me back then that calcium deficiency resolves itself in just a few months, so a broken ankle all those years later could not have been caused by malnutrition. But I didn't register that objection because, as a typical victim, I perceived the connection as logical.

I only broke away from that type of thinking on the day I was able to forgive the Nazis. Since then, when something happens to me, I no longer connect it to Auschwitz.

Of course I also have some delayed effects from my time in the camp, but I have crossed present-day falls off the list.

What makes this mentality dangerous is that a victim always stays a victim. And then finds daily mental validation, "See? I told you. That only happens to me." It's a vicious cycle.

And the bad thing is that it causes victims to label themselves as such. No one else is forcing them into lifelong slavery.

There is one way to break free from the chains. But it can't be done simply by resolving to be free at last. First, it's crucial to release the people from your life who want to make you a victim. Hitler, for example, still haunts the thoughts and fears of people who were persecuted in the Second World War. They are filled with rage and hatred for Hitler and the Nazis, even seventy years later. As old-timers! And they ask me, embittered, "How can you possibly forgive, Eva?"

These people cannot conceive of the fact that I am through with this past era. They cannot conceive of all the goodness that becomes possible simply by letting the past go.

I use my strength to drive away the burden of remembering. And yet, people who take my advice do not suffer from amnesia. They know exactly what happened back then. But remembering no longer keeps them down.

It becomes just one part of who they are.

That is why, in 1995, I founded the CANDLES Holocaust Museum and Education Center in Terre Haute, Indiana, which more than one hundred thousand people have visited since then.

It's about making a statement that draws on memory.

Sadly, many survivors have misunderstood my approach. And many Jews have wanted nothing to do with me.

It remains unthinkable for them to forgive the Nazis. And baffling.

Nevertheless.

I am a strong-willed person.

My will to live was incredible. Even though everyone was against me. And even though very few people helped me.

I don't know where this strong will came from. Perhaps it is a gift, a genetic peculiarity; perhaps it is a result of my father saying no to me, challenging me, so that from a young age I was practiced at handling that challenge. But I am inclined to see that will as something I was born with.

Already, when I was a little girl, my family used to say, "Eva, you've got pepper and paprika in your veins. There's something particular about you. Something special."

And early on I already know that if something happened somewhere, I wouldn't watch from the sidelines—I'd be jumping around in the eye of the hurricane. And, in general, that meant *trouble*.

⁎ ⁎ ⁎

"What can I do?"

I received a letter from a woman who had been raped. She wanted to forgive, but felt incapable of it.

I contemplated how to respond to this woman. After her recuperation.

First, she'd need to ask herself whether she wants to continue being a victim of her circumstances for any longer. That's important. Only when she's ready can she make a conscious decision to stop being a victim.

I told her the following in my reply:

> Get out a piece of paper and a pen. Then write a letter to the perpetrator. Put down everything that comes to mind. Seriously, everything!
>
> But at the end, add one simple sentence: I forgive you.
>
> And you have to really mean those words.
>
> That moment is when you find out how tightly you're still tied up in the process. First you need to break free of your rage.
>
> But never, ever, send that letter to the perpetrator. What you have written is only for you. It embodies your personality and simultaneously brings about your emotional healing—all that though a bunch of curly cursive letters.
>
> And the moment you forgive and feel free, you will experience a tremendous sense of peace. So why not

sing, dance, and rejoice that the enormous burden has been lifted?

And what if that's not how you feel? If you don't manage to forgive?

Then write the letter again.

And again.

There's no limit. Maybe you need to write it ten times, maybe twenty. You might even need to write a hundred letters.

Most people desire something entirely different in a moment like that. Rather than longing for forgiveness, they wish the most awful things in the world on the perpetrator. They wish for him to be tarred and feathered, to have an accident, and to roast in hell!

Instead, I say, you need to reach a point at which you really no longer wish any harm on the other person.

But there's one more crucial point: never send the letter to the other person. No matter what you do. Not even to show that you have gotten over them.

I've seen this often with couples. One time, a wife sent a letter of forgiveness to her ex-husband. She wanted to demonstrate that she had moved on from the divorce and, most of all, moved on from him. And that she wasn't interested in him anymore. But by sending the letter at all, she demonstrated that she still had plenty of baggage. And then, of course, he sent a reply straight back presenting matters from his viewpoint, "I will forgive you too for your court testimony that got me thrown in jail for four years. And ruined my life."

I asked the woman, "Did you really want to set that kind of spiral in motion? This will never end between the two of you. Neither your relationship, nor your endless accusations, recriminations, and justifications."

"You're right," she answered. "I just wanted to show him how strong I am."

"Don't show him anything," I said. "You know how you feel. You know that you don't feel any rage anymore. You're no longer caught up in this carousel of emotions. You don't want to invest any more emotions in this."

A victim has the right to be free, but it's impossible to be free without shaking off this daily burden of pain and rage.

If all you can do anymore is cry, does that help? Or are you crying out of self-pity? In Auschwitz, crying wasn't much of a solution. As a ten-year-old, I cried because I needed my mother, because I was hungry, shivering, fearful, sick—but only briefly. And then I was done. I could have used up my last energy reserves in the process. Crying is incompatible with survival. If I wanted to live, I couldn't cry. That hasn't changed. People who lose themselves in tears, simply lose.

It's invaluable to focus on all the beautiful things in life rather than on what is painful or dysfunctional at a given moment. You should at least make an effort to concentrate more on the good things than on the bad things.

I don't mean to say that I've never cried. When my son got sick with cancer, for example, and I drove for an hour to the hospital at six o'clock every morning, I cried the whole way there. I was constantly asking myself, "Why did my son have to get cancer?"

And yet he never once saw me cry. At his bedside, I cheered him up and gave off optimistic energy. He probably could never have dreamed that I was crying so much.

But I was—privately. Because it hurt and I didn't know what to do to counter all that pain. In the end, he triumphed over his cancer, and he is healthy now. He became a doctor himself in Milwaukee, Wisconsin. But back then I knew that he needed my strength and my positive aura in order to sense that everything would be all right again.

It's quite a feat, but anyone can do it with a little practice.

Here's something else you can practice. The next time you want to drown in tears, try instead to think about something that makes you feel good. That takes a lot of effort, I know. But in Auschwitz it was a bitter necessity. After a while, you'll get so good at it that you'll become an advocate for others. You'll help them by giving them hope and strength.

Actually, it's very easy to become a victim. It doesn't take any extra work. It happens to me even to this day.

And over and over, it comes down to this: How do you get out of a messy situation?

A victim is ceaselessly preoccupied only with what once befell him. And he rationalizes it without end. Doing this makes no sense to the people around him, but for the victim it's immensely beneficial. At least superficially.

This thinking draws a direct causative arrow from something that happened far in the past to a broken ankle in the present.

Will you somehow break free on your own from this mentality of constantly repeating "poor me"?

The answer is no.

Not on your own, not just like that. We remain entangled in it for life.

Because there's one more thing victims enjoy. They like it when others feel sympathy for them. Or empathy.

Sympathy is truly a very pleasant thing—but it doesn't solve the problem.

How long will you thrive for if people only show their empathy for you?

If you're stranded in the desert, dying of thirst and almost starving, frantic for water, then sympathy won't get you anywhere.

Ultimately, you need to get out of the desert.

Each day, children are raped and abused somewhere in the world. Their biggest dream is to get away from that terrifying place. But when all they're offered is sympathy, maybe some money in compensation, that's not enough. These children will continue to carry their pain inside them. Every single day, they suffer again from what happened to them.

Pure sympathy doesn't get them anywhere.

This kind of solicitude makes children wither away as lifelong victims. "It was so awful. It was terrible." That's all true! But it doesn't pull the children out of that mentality of "poor me."

You also need to get rid of such self-pity inside you. Instead, repeat to yourself: "I am a valuable human being with the right to be free. What has been imposed on me?"

Tell yourself, "I have every right to live. I don't need to apologize for my feelings. Likewise, I won't accept sympathy from others because I don't need it."

Then you will receive the energy to heal yourself.

Let me emphasize one more time: To forgive means more than to "let go." It means becoming active. No longer being passive. We accidentally become victims when a person or organization robs us of the power to continue using our minds and bodies as we see fit.

Instead, something was done to us that put us in a position of powerlessness. Similarly, the deliberate choice to forgive helps us to experience healing and liberation. And to live self-sufficiently again.

Otherwise, that whole pattern can end badly.

Take the story of another Auschwitz survivor. A very embittered man. He told me, "You know, I always carry two guns in my car, all day. One under my seat and another one in the trunk."

I asked him why.

He replied, "In case I run into a denier or a former Nazi . . . so I can blow his brains out."

He mistrusted the political system, the police, society, and was suspicious of everybody. He couldn't believe that the world had any good people left in it. He said, "I was alone in Auschwitz, and I survived alone."

This man had to fight out the bitter hardships of an Auschwitz survivor on his own. He saw himself in the middle of an eternal cycle of eat or be eaten. Where no one was trustworthy. Ever. And where no one could expect anyone ever to offer help unselfishly.

All he could still manage was a desperate attempt to survive. Who could blame him?

Luckily, I had my twin sister in Auschwitz. She was at my side every day and helped me to *still* believe in human values.

A significant difference.

It's a big problem when survivors get older and older, burdened by increasing health problems, and then face, like the icing on the cake, their psychological problems. It's horrible for them to feel like victims—without an inkling that it's possible to free themselves. By deciding to forgive the Nazis, they could lead better lives again.

⁂

Many victims say, "I can't accept what happened."

An understandable thought.

But it *did* happen.

It can't be undone.

So there are only two possibilities left. Either you shorten your remaining lifespan on a mad quest to become a photocopy of the perpetrator. And ruin your life in the process. And while you're at it, the decision will also lead to you ruining other people's lives.

Or you can say to yourself, I'm so grateful that I'm still alive, that I can feel, smell, breathe. And that I can enjoy my life.

Those are the only two options.

Forgiveness helps keep me from becoming the kind of person who emulates the perpetrator. Who becomes evil. That's because putting yourself on the perpetrator's level will only bring difficulties.

It's a trap.

Perpetrators need to be punished—that's another point—but I refuse to be drawn into the question of the punishment's severity.

Because rage makes a person evil.

Where do all these crazy problems in the world come from? Someone has been hurt, demands gratification and revenge, so he strikes back, causing new pain, which again cries for retribution—a hamster wheel of lunacy that spins faster and faster. A cycle of destruction. Until the whole world is full of victims.

Because we teach the wrong lessons.

"Never forgive" is one such lesson that we pass on from generation to generation.

It's a trap.

Because killing starts with hatred. And hatred, in its smoldering core, is keen to kill.

I will not permit myself to hate.

Because I found out, since I have been more and more occupied with the idea of forgiveness, that even pronouncing the word "hatred" carries a load of destructive energy. I remember watching my kids tossing another child around. They were playing a pretty rough game. You couldn't see a trace of friendliness left on their faces. This is all even worse with hatred. When you look at a hate-filled person—his facial expression, the stance of his body—you can see every aspect of him tensing up into a malicious gesture.

Many people don't like focusing too much on this dark side, but since I've been thinking about forgiveness, I've been forced to look into the other side of the coin. So, what does it mean to hate?

If you decide to hate, it essentially means that you are prepared to destroy yourself. Because hatred is destructive at its core.

It doesn't inspire a good feeling in anyone else. Instead, it produces destructive bodily reactions.

If only people could understand that! They damage themselves much more than they damage the person they hate.

Or have you ever seen a hate-filled person who seemed content or happy?

It's actually quite simple. If you focus on destroying something you don't like, directing all your thoughts and efforts toward the best way to obliterate it, it's only logical that this destructive energy will bring devastation to your own thoughts and efforts.

I don't know a single positive thing that has come out of hate. Not one thing!

When kids play at shooting each other with toy guns, it doesn't seem harmonious to me. Their faces don't look nice, in my opinion. On the other hand, a child interacting with an animal, for example, appears so friendly and positive. Animals are a perfect therapeutic option for children who have been deeply wounded. Flowers, too—wonderful. Especially when they bloom. Caring for plants, making sure they grow and thrive, opens up the heart. It's a magnificent feeling to gaze at a beautiful flower in all its glory. The colors, the perfection, incredible!

By the way, a person who is occupied with destruction and hatred every day will never experience those feelings.

It's enough for me even to read about evil things.

On the other hand, it quickly stirs me up when I hear about people helping other people. That's marvelous!

Stories like that allow me to believe again that people are good at heart. Sometimes, a constructive episode like that can keep me in a good mood for days.

For me, the point is not to protect myself from all bad news and only look at the positive. I read as much news as possible and I hear about all kinds of developments. But I try hard not to be affected by the news. I take it in, but I try not to integrate into my heart or my memory.

Things happen. Period.

That isn't easy when I hear about refugees. News like that strikes a nerve in me. Not to have a country, no property, not even a pillow—and instead to be on the run day and night. It's appalling.

Many people these days are more preoccupied with what's currently "in." Or what's in style. How unimportant!

One time I was in New York to be photographed for *Vanity Fair* magazine.

"What will you be wearing?" one such stylist asked me.

"I'll be wearing 'Eva Kor,'" I replied.

"Oh," said the young woman, distraught. "Do you seriously mean you'll be wearing this polyester jacket? *No way!*"

And she rolled over a cart loaded down with various outfits, and another young woman devoted herself to describing all the labels and materials to me. Both of them were very intent on finding something appropriate for me. But I hated all of it. That wasn't my world.

Eventually, I told the young woman, "Listen. It's not about what I wear and what you can make out of me. Clothing won't make any of us important. Do you really think that just because you wrap yourself in a few square inches of designer fabric, you're suddenly a somebody? Not if you ask me. What's more important to me is what someone does with their mind and their heart."

In the end, I was photographed in my blue jacket.

The way I like myself. The way I actually look.

Anyone who knows me knows I'm a simple woman who can make do with little. I am at peace with myself. I'm not jittery. I don't try to change or convert the world or other people.

Many people hop around nervously. They don't know who they are or where they want to be.

My only advice is to make friends with yourself because you can't be anyone else. And don't be upset if other people don't like you or what you do—just be honest with yourself.

So if people reject you because you don't wear designer clothes, accept it. Life can't just be about impressing other people. Unfortunately, there are plenty of people who classify others by what they wear. If you can't afford to purchase some of those overpriced rags, you're worthless in their eyes.

Nevertheless.

⋆ ⋆ ⋆

Forgiveness is a lifelong process. We need to practice it again and again.

But many people run out of steam along the way.

Writing or reading about it is much, much easier than actually practicing it. That's why I always advise that if you're determined to forgive, don't satisfy yourself with a resolution. Grab a piece of paper and write down everything that is wounding you. Because you need to get past the pain.

An unbelievable amount of pain lurks in people who have been abused. You first need to acknowledge that "Yes, indeed. This crime has severely wounded me. But from now on, I want to be free of it. To achieve that goal, I need to get certain things done."

Writing things down is not about making some kind of philosophical statement. If you forgive—from the bottom of your heart, not under your breath—you will experience a healing energy. You will feel all the weight lifted from your shoulders. All the horrible things that have befallen you, (which you constantly see in your mind's eye: *Who* did *what*, and *how?*) together with those atrocious memories, none of them pleasant in the least. With forgiveness, they all disappear.

And on top of that, you gain back power over your life.

No one ever asked you if you wanted to be a victim. But one hallmark of victimhood is that victims no longer have any say-so over their own lives. Certain people can treat you however they feel like. And you can't stop the mob of your enemies in its tracks.

When those people leave, the awful memories remain. But that can be changed—if you forgive.

Afterward, don't go digging through your memories anymore. You're finished with that. The past can't be reconstructed in hindsight, so don't go digging and mining. This part is especially difficult for many people. Including me.

Maybe a little anecdote will help. About twenty years ago, when I opened CANDLES Holocaust Museum in Terre Haute, a reporter interviewed me about my plans. "What can you do with the $10,000.00 of donations" was her first question.

I thought that was impertinent. Throughout the interview, she seemed extremely hostile to me. Her eyes seem to be saying that my ideas for a small-town Holocaust museum were naïve. A plan that could never work.

It bugged me.

And in all the years that followed, whenever I saw her, that skeptical look flashed before my eyes.

At some point, I'd had enough. When I was awarded a prize for my museum, I took the reporter aside and said that I'd forgiven her, too.

Except the woman had no idea what I was talking about. She could hardly even remember that first interview. Instead, she racked her brains to think of what in the world might have happened in that conversation.

All of that came about because I couldn't stop digging in the past. An image had therefore solidified in my mind that had aggravated me more and more.

That was my lesson. I thought, *Good Lord, Eva. How stupid can you be?* Why hadn't I just let go of it all immediately after that first interview, even during it?

Simply forgive.

Because when you forgive, you release the only energy that you really have at your disposal.

And to forgive someone who once planned to kill you releases enormous energy. I can tell you that much. It's also the final link between perpetrator and victim. And the fact that you are holding the reins gives you a sense of power over the perpetrator. You no longer feel helplessly subjected to the pain that no revenge, no death sentence could ever soothe.

Forgiveness frees us from the pain of the past. I understand that it might also be a gift to the perpetrator. But bearing the pain alone doesn't help me either.

⚡ ⚡ ⚡

"And what if I have recurring nightmares every night?"

I've been asked that many times.

I had most of my nightmares in Romania. Later, in Israel, I hardly had any. Because all of my neighbors there, the street sweeper, the doctor, the police officer, every soldier, everyone was Jewish. I was no longer threatened by my environment.

That was a critical reason my life took a turn for the better. And why I became the person I am. I experienced being Jewish as something positive.

We all need to experience who we are. As a positive experience. We can't be anyone else.

If your environment reacts to you negatively—whether it's your beliefs, your opinions, or your appearance—then you won't like yourself. But you have to learn to like yourself because otherwise you can't become a good human being. Everything hangs on your self-acceptance.

Before I lived in Israel, every single experience I had of being Jewish was horrible. Being a Jew was potentially lethal.

In Israel, on the contrary, it was a joy to be Jewish. To this day, I have all kinds of wonderful memories of when I was there. One time, Miriam had a date with a boy who wouldn't take no for an answer. She was very aggravated about it when she got home. I told her, "Call the guy up and tell him you want to go to the movies—and I'll go on the date instead of you."

No sooner said than done.

I put on Miriam's skirt and blouse and made my way there. I didn't want to worry about how I'd recognize the fellow, so I went early. The young man saw me, thought I was Miriam, and huddled right up. He said he'd already bought the tickets.

I purred, "By the way, my roommate isn't home tonight, just so you know . . ."

I knew what would happen next. His face instantly changed and he whispered, "The movie is nothing special. Let's see your apartment."

So we went back. When I opened the door, Miriam got in position. When the man entered behind me and saw Miriam waiting there, he stood in shock for at least ten minutes. One look at Miriam, then at me. And then back. Finally, we told him, "If a girl says no to you, you should be enough of a gentleman to accept that no means no. I hope you've learned your lesson."

That was fun.

And those happy experiences made it a little easier for me to move to the US. I lived off of those memories. After that, I wasn't usually as upset when other kids taunted my son or my daughter. By that point, I liked myself on the whole—and I felt secure about my religion.

However, if you don't feel safe, you will react very strangely. In other words, if you live in an environment where you can't break free of your nightmares, moving certainly might help. In my case, it even saved my life. If I hadn't, the climate of fear and insecurity in Romania would have destroyed me.

✻ ✻ ✻

I recently received a similar letter.

"I don't know why," one woman wrote, "but my parents have mistreated me my whole life. I'm the elder one. My younger sister got everything she wanted. My childhood bedroom never even had heating. Now my younger sister lives with her husband in another city, and my mother is there too, on her deathbed. I'm contemplating visiting my mother one last time. But when I think about my childhood, I don't know what to do anymore."

I wrote back, "I have no idea what happened, of course. I also have no idea why you were treated so badly, but it's certainly not your fault. No child should be treated that way. However, there is no way to force people to treat us as we'd like to be treated. The only thing you have control over is your own behavior.

"In my opinion, parents like that are neither role models nor caregivers. They aren't good people, but that doesn't mean you cannot become a good person despite that. And a role model in your own right. You have recognized that what was done to you was wrong. You didn't deserve it, and it wasn't your fault. Ultimately, though, you should forgive your parents. So that you can move on and feel good as the person you are. Write a letter to your parents."

Yet I forgot to emphasize—but don't send the letter on any account!

So the inevitable happened. A few weeks later, I received the following note back, "I sent the letter to my mother and my sister, and now they're both laughing at me."

I called the woman right away and told her I was very, very sorry about all of this. "I should have told you more clearly. Never send it! These sorts of people have their own opinions about what happened and you will never be able to change those opinions."

"But I wanted to see my mother before she dies . . ."

"Unfortunately, I can't help you with that," I said. "There's only one thing you can do, as always: forgive. From the bottom of your heart. That's the only power you have over your family. Take that power seriously. Don't joke about it in the slightest. I understand you very well. You wish you had a loving mother. I'm sorry to tell you this, but you never did and you never will. And no one can change that state of affairs. Accept that. Not because it was your fault—it wasn't—but because it's a fact. You can't change these things. No one can. But nevertheless, tell yourself that you're a valuable person. Because you are! And if you still want to do something, then improve yourself. Fix everything in your life that is in your power to fix."

The woman was silent.

"If you want to see your dying mother again, but your mother would rather stay in contact with your younger sister, there's nothing you can do about it. You sent them both the letter because you wanted to show your family that you are no longer consumed by the past. And that you are so noble as to forgive everyone. But that was not an act of generosity. You wanted to demonstrate plenty of things to your family, but not necessarily forgiveness. You wanted to be happy with your own life at last. But the desire to manipulate the toxic side of your family is only causing new problems in yourself. And now you are reacting to their reactions. You don't need that. You could have lived just fine without those reactions.

"All of us can only control our own behavior and our own feelings. And that's what we should concentrate on.

"On finding friends. Start a self-help group. Enrich your friendships. But please don't fall back into those poisonous relationships that weren't your doing.

"There are plenty of people who were extremely abused by their own families. I don't have an inkling why that happens, let alone why your parents don't appreciate you, but it's more common than we can imagine."

My concept of forgiveness does not require a detour by way of psychotherapy, though by no means do I rule out such methods. It can be an enriching opportunity for many people—if it leads to the same outcome. Which is being the master of your own life again. Feeling energy for your own life again. Meeting new friends, developing new interests, and communicating with other people whom you can help with their difficulties.

If you can do that, you will realize what *power* lies in forgiveness. You can use that energy to help others. That is important to me because the world is full of wounded, broken people.

None of them was born wounded or broken. But all of those people were shaped in their earliest childhoods.

Anywhere in the world, our own family is our first school. And at the same time, it is our first path of pain.

There are a number of reasons people persist in victimhood. One is that they are afraid they will have nothing left if they let go of their rage against the perpetrator. Rage has become part of their identities. But in the end, they feel as though their strength and their control over their lives has been stolen from them.

Some people truly believe that the only way for them to gain control of their fear is by clinging tightly to their rage.

But that's not true.

For one thing, they aren't giving up the right to be enraged. They are still allowed to fly off the handle if they want to. I personally have exchanged rage for the resolution not to be enraged. After all, rage is purely negative and supports destructive impulses. It isn't beneficial for our psyches or for our mental health, and it doesn't lead anywhere. It would be very difficult to find any constructive argument in favor of rage, and virtually impossible for a person to act out his fury without harming himself or others.

Again and again, I try to convince people that giving up anger and rage is a wonderful decision for the body and mind. You exchange the small satisfaction of a tantrum for the great contentment of freedom. In fact, if I lay out the choice for people, I've never encountered anyone who would truly prefer hatred and rage to feelings of joy and happiness.

We have to understand that just because we've outwardly escaped a threatening situation, that doesn't mean the problem has gone away. Many people keep returning to the starting point of their mental wound because that feeling simulates a type of familiarity.

If all your thoughts revolve around getting the perpetrator into prison (or even worse), you yourself become an executioner. Personally, I don't want anything to do with that kind of job.

If we used only half of the energy that we waste on our preoccupation with the perpetrators on helping victims instead, this world would take a giant leap forward. Not to mention the risk that victims will pass on their repressed rage and powerlessness to their own children and grandchildren, who, in turn, eventually seek revenge against the children or grandchildren of the perpetrators. This creates a never-ending vicious cycle.

A survivor is not at all to blame, and equally I am not responsible for getting the perpetrator behind bars. Instead, I consider it my duty as a survivor to be the best Eva I can possibly be.

And people who forgive have made peace with themselves— and give the gift of peace to the world. At the very least, that is my sincere hope.

> ✶ ✶ ✶

As I said, I can't change what has happened. I can only change my attitude toward it.

I can't change the perpetrator either. But by *not* going berserk—the predictable response that the perpetrator seeks—I bring about the best retribution.

I also like to call it a "gift to myself." Allow me to quote Desmond Tutu, an Anglican archbishop and a moral authority in South Africa. He played a central role in fighting Apartheid, and wrote this about forgiveness:

> There were so many nights when I, as a young boy, had to watch helplessly as my father verbally and physically

abused my mother. . . . My father has long since died, but if I could speak to him today, I would want to tell him that I had forgiven him. Why would I do such a thing? I know it is the only way to heal the pain in my boyhood heart. . . . Forgiveness is not dependent on the actions of others. . . . We don't forgive to help the other person. We don't forgive for others. We forgive for ourselves. Forgiveness, in other words, is the best form of self-interest.

The only way to experience healing and peace is to forgive. Until we can forgive, we remain locked in our pain and locked out of the possibility of experiencing healing and freedom, locked out of the possibility of being at peace.

Sometimes people send me letters asking how they can manage to forgive their spouses.

On this topic, I tend to be more reserved.

A partnership is one of the most demanding challenges a person can rise to. I don't believe so many people actually realize what they are taking on. Being in love, the "honeymoon period," is marvelous, but unfortunately it passes fairly quickly.

And although I have advice about almost every sphere of life, I hold back on the subject of partnership. Because it's an experience we all need to have for ourselves. The challenge is that most of us are unaware of the extent to which we cede our independence when we get married. And hardly anyone fully realizes in advance what this "theft of freedom" will entail.

If I were to describe an ideal partner, I'd say that he or she should maintain his or her independence while valuing the other partner's independence in turn. And he or she should appreciate the kind of person his or her partner was before marriage.

Nobody needs a partner to be happy. The truth is that another person won't make you happy if you weren't already.

So respect your partner's independence.

The other thing I'd recommend is to have fun together. Do something you know your partner will enjoy. Your partner should likewise act on a suggestion that would bring you gratification. If you share experiences based on joy, you will cement a solid foundation. The ideal of a good marriage rests on a very close friendship with mutual respect—and love will automatically follow.

If these conditions are in place, feelings of caring—and, in turn, of love—will rise to the surface.

Difficulties always emerge when one partner becomes ill, requiring a large amount of consolation and assistance, and the other one needs to give support. This issue will come up in almost all partnerships sooner or later. How will you handle it? I can only advise that you don't overextend yourself with care and help. Find out how your partner wants to be cared for. Does your partner need a lot of attention when he or she is sick, or is your partner satisfied to know that you're within reach?

No matter what, the subject of forgiveness plays a major role in partnership. In such an intimate connection, people are easily hurt. So if someone hurts your feelings, you should talk to your partner as soon as possible, or else your wounds will bubble up as though on a hot stove. Talk to each other! And afterward, make the decision again to forgive. Always. Because it's good for you and good for your partnership.

Particularly when the other person has done something wrong, and even if he or she isn't willing to apologize. Most of all, if the other person feels he or she is justified. You will notice how good for you it is to forgive and that it heals you. You will also see your partner soften.

In a close partnership, it is very easy to hurt each other's feelings, especially among people who are caring for each other.

People commonly say, "If you loved me, you'd know . . ."

But that's not true in the least!

No one can read another person's mind, not even when two people love each other very much and finish each other's sentences. So don't listen to that logic. You need to talk to each other about your thoughts, feelings, and ideas. And if it goes badly, forgive.

Over and over and over.

I see forgiveness as the summit of a very high mountain.

One face is dark, bleak, damp, and very hard to climb. But those who go through the struggle to reach the summit can see the beauty of the mountain's other face, which is full of flowers, doves, butterflies, and sunshine. When we stand on the summit, we can see both sides of the mountain.

And forgiveness gets you through any situation.

In this book, by the way, I only want to write about myself and my path, not about what my family and friends think about it. It's no secret that they don't always share my views. But I respect theirs.

My husband, for instance, did not talk about his camp experiences for decades, not even with his own children. He has a different personality.

That only changed in 1997, two years after he retired. And two years after I'd opened my museum. Back then the museum was even smaller because I didn't have the cash for the whole building. Where the lecture hall is now, there used to be a travel agency. It wasn't the perfect solution, but it was the only way for me to open a room commemorating my sister Miriam. It also finally gave me a place to do interviews. With the photos in the background, it was immediately clear what we were talking about. We didn't have to cover the basics as much anymore.

By two years after the opening, the little museum was well received. Visitors streamed in and teachers signed up to visit with their classes. My husband helped me two days a week whenever a group of schoolchildren was visiting and took care of the office work. Considering how critical he was at first about the idea of such a museum, he soon grew very involved.

Because I still had a full-time job in real estate at the time, the museum was only open to the public for three hours on Saturdays. In 1997, a teacher had signed up to visit the museum with a class of gifted and talented kids. I couldn't be there that day because of a real estate appointment. But I told the teacher to come anyway. After all, I knew my husband would be there—my husband, who had never spoken publicly about his past. I also knew very well that he loved smart children. So I fervently hoped they would ask him some equally smart questions.

When the day arrived, I didn't explain to Mickey what was about to happen. So he opened the doors, let in the school group, and planned to stand quietly in the background as usual. But suddenly, one boy came up to him and said, "Mr. Kor, you are the unluckiest person I've ever seen in my life."

Mickey was taken aback. "What makes you say that?"

"Well, you were in Europe when Hitler came to power. That definitely wasn't a lucky time. And now you're living near the wrong football team."

My husband began to laugh hysterically. And from that moment on, the teenagers were able to ask him whatever they liked.

It was the first day since his liberation that he spoke openly about his survival.

This experience was important for me, too. It showed me once again that everything we do, even the smallest action, has a ripple effect. It touches the lives of many other people—and has tremendous ramifications.

5

How Can You Forgive?

The moment I agreed to testify against a former SS junior squad leader, who had been employed in Auschwitz from 1942 to 1944, in a trial in Germany, I had a strange feeling of uncertainty. The man, Oskar Gröning, was accused of complicity to murder in 300,000 cases by the district court of Lüneburg. In the German press, he was dubbed the "Bookkeeper of Auschwitz" because he dealt with the money that the people had stored in their clothing or bags when they arrived at the camp.

Gröning counted and recorded the money and stacked the bills in a steel cabinet. In 1978, he was interrogated as a suspect for the first time, but the proceedings were halted in 1985. That's why the renewed charges were limited to the so-called Hungarian deportation. In this time, from May 16 to July 11, 1944, the SS deported approximately 425,000 Hungarian Jews to Auschwitz. At least 300,000 people were immediately killed in the gas chambers. And Gröning was often standing on the ramp when the trains arrived.

I spoke with my museum employees about what would happen in such a large-scale trial. We quickly realized that you cannot plan ahead or predict anything in a trial like this. Especially when it comes to my reaction when a Nazi suddenly enters the room.

No matter what transpired between me and this man, it would definitely happen spontaneously. That is the purest form of human communication—without a strategy, without a goal, without ulterior motives. Just two people reacting to each other.

Once I had arrived in Germany, I was supposed to testify after a long list of people, but for reasons I am unaware of, I was suddenly the first to testify. The entire process was quite disorganized, so I decided that since I had the opportunity to testify, I would take it.

I was quite surprised when the people in the courtroom suddenly applauded after my testimony was finished. My lawyer said he had never seen anything like that before. The judge demanded quiet in the courtroom, as this was not an entertainment show, where people could clap whenever they wanted to, and I completely agreed with him. But at the same time, I was proud of having the opportunity to testify in this important case. Afterward, many people came to me, crying, and they told me they had never heard about the events on the selection ramp before and what it means to be separated from your family all of a sudden.

I stayed in the courtroom because I wanted to hear what Gröning had to say about the whole thing. But all he said on record was that Auschwitz was very well organized, particularly during the selections.

I was indignant because that just wasn't true!

Yet I suspect that he only wanted to truthfully depict the parts of his testimony that wouldn't endanger him. Or maybe he was simply a ninety-three-year-old man who pieced together his memories of the past the way he would like to believe it.

He likewise said in his testimony that he didn't kill anyone but was simply a "small cog in the greater machinery." I wonder (and I still wonder today) what would have happened if one had removed one of these so-called "small cogs" from the machinery?

My answer is that "the machine" would have stopped working. That is precisely the way a death factory works—and he, Gröning, most definitely supported this apparatus in his role.

So I had to struggle to stay in my seat.

At one point the word *justice* was even used—a word that is absurd to use in connection with Auschwitz. Even if you were to hang every single Nazi, would it achieve justice? It wouldn't bring back one single member of my family.

At the same time, neo-Nazis were demonstrating in front of the courtroom. I wanted to go outside and talk with these people. I wanted to ask them, "What is your problem?"

But when I went outside, the police had already escorted the group to a separate area, and none of the officers wanted to tell me where they were. I thought this went a little far. Quite a large number of officers had been deployed, so I think the neo-

Nazis couldn't have posed a real threat. But the police would not be swayed.

And I can guarantee you—I may be an old woman, not very tall and not very sure on my feet, but I would have confronted those Fascists.

When I went back to the courtroom, I suddenly found myself in an adjoining room where Oskar Gröning was sitting. I froze.

At the same time, I had the impulse to approach him. He was sitting on a wooden chair with his back to me, so he only recognized me at the last minute. I approached him from the side, without the faintest idea what I wanted from him, but suddenly Gröning turned to me and stood up.

I wanted to shake his hand, but he grabbed my left hand and wouldn't let go. He clutched me tightly. Then I realized he was turning white as a sheet and that his circulatory system was about to collapse. His head was hanging to the side and he was about to fall. But he was still clutching my hand tightly. I know about circulatory collapses myself—they can happen to me when I stand up too fast. I realized what was happening, but I couldn't hold him up.

Gröning was a large man, quite thin, but still much heavier than I. And he was holding my hand. At that moment, he was no longer a Nazi to me, but an elderly man. The human element had triumphed again. Although he was a Nazi, I still wouldn't let him fall on the floor. So I began to scream, "Help, help!" and someone immediately came to my aid and stopped his fall. It was better that way since otherwise I probably would have fallen on top of him as well.

Not even in my wildest dreams had I imagined our first encounter like this.

When he had recovered, I wanted to have a photo taken with Gröning. I am a sentimental person. There was no other day when a photo could have been taken.

I said to my lawyer, "Here is my camera, please take a photo."

As I walked over to Gröning, he wanted to stand up again. "No, please stay seated! Let's not repeat the same scenario again."

So Gröning remained seated, but while the photo was being taken, he suddenly pulled me close and gave me a kiss on both cheeks. It was so fast that I couldn't even comprehend what was happening. It was somehow so innocent, so genuine. He did so because he liked me. There was no other motive. What other motive could there have been?

This man suddenly kissed me? I thought. I was confused. How was I supposed to deal with that? Should I be angry?

Oskar Gröning didn't want to hurt me, he didn't want to hit me, he had simply demonstrated to me in a clumsy way that he liked me.

I still do not know what the right response would have been. But the world saw this photo and complained, "Eva Kor Mozes is kissing a Nazi! How could she?!" However, my critics don't know the important background story. And they aren't interested in the deeper symbolism—of an old man whose deeds afflict him and who cannot find another way to demonstrate that to me.

As I said, you cannot tell what will happen when a victim and perpetrator meet on the level of pure human connection. I think that it would have been wrong to yell, "You devil!" in his face.

We are both human beings. What would we have learned from such an outburst? What would we have been able to tell each other? I didn't meet Gröning in order to make accusations, and he didn't touch me in order to hurt me. We were simply two people who hoped to still feel each other somehow.

Of course it would have been very, very helpful to me if Oskar Gröning had given a statement about his time in Auschwitz. Unfortunately, he still has not done so.

⁕ ⁕ ⁕

This silence reverberates through the generations, dividing them.

These acts remain rooted in people's bodies and souls, and they are passed on all the way to the grandchildren's generation. Every challenge that we face, every dark spot that we repress and do not examine in daylight continues to grow like a tumor. In turn, the generations walk on eggshells with each other, thinking to themselves, *Just don't say the wrong thing.*

However, when we shed light on these dark spots, we can remove them and break them down into their individual components. That's why my museum bears the motto, "CANDLES Holocaust Museum and Education Center shines a light on the story of the Holocaust and Eva Kor to illuminate the world with hope, healing, respect, and responsibility."

Sadly, I sometimes have the feeling that even my fellow Jews do not completely understand what I'm trying to say. Judaism is a very old religion, and as far as I know, it was the first religion to profess one god. The Jews were among the first to develop an advanced civilization of reading and writing. Their writings offered the world a vision of a peaceful world for the first time.

It would be amazing to me if the Jews of the world could now teach people to heal. Through forgiveness.

At the moment, however, I have the feeling that neither the rabbis nor the Israeli politicians want to forgive the Nazis.

Forgiving one's friends is very easy. The challenge is to forgive one's worst enemies. If you can forgive these people, then you will manage to forgive everyone else. Francis Maitland Balfour, a Scottish zoologist, said in the late nineteenth century, "The best thing you can give to your enemy is forgiveness . . . to yourself, respect." Sadly, that is often no more than a noble desire.

Yet, it would wake up people all over the world, it would force a new kind of attention to the countless battlefields of the world—when, of all people, the Jews would forgive the Nazis.

As crazy as it sounds, I want the world to live in peace. That's the reason behind my ceaseless work and efforts with every means available to me.

Shortly after my testimony in the Gröning trial, the first critics spoke up. In a public statement, the forty-nine other joint plaintiffs demonstrated that I stood alone. I was also accused of being a "traitor" or "unreasonable." In particular, my appearance on a German TV talk show was criticized internationally as a "public performance," even by former Auschwitz victims who weren't involved in the Gröning trial at all. Of course it's completely acceptable if they want to criticize me. But there is one thing that I find upsetting, and that's when my critics address me indirectly via the press or my attorneys.

I would prefer a personal discussion. I get in touch with them and plead for dialogue again and again, but I still don't have the impression that my critics are particularly concerned with speaking with me directly. I think we would have a much better idea of each other's perspectives if we talked directly to each other. Face-to-face. Perhaps we would even find we have common interests.

I am not their enemy, and I do not like it when my critics have the feeling that I am their opponent. These confrontations make no sense to me. But what should I do? It makes me uneasy to read reports in which they are increasingly annoyed with me.

I am a survivor, just like they are. And I think that our shared background means we have a lot in common that we could talk about in a familiar setting. Having a conversation face-to-face should always take priority. Just like the personal encounter I had with Oskar Gröning.

In these moments, something happens that cannot be predicted. And the same thing could happen in encounters among us survivors who have different points of view.

However, the situation at the moment has taken a rather sad turn. Should I really become the enemy of other survivors? And, by the same token, should I really turn these people into my enemies?

That's absurd. We should have the same goals in life. Maybe we don't think the same way, but that's all the more reason for us to sit down together. I firmly believe that there is more that unites us than divides us.

Many of the things I have been accused of are in fact untrue. For example, many people criticize me for appearing on a German talk show during the Oskar Gröning trial and supposedly declaring that all criminal prosecutions against Nazis should be stopped.

That is not true! To reiterate, I have never advocated for prosecutions to be stopped. On the contrary—I even told Oskar Gröning that he should encourage all other Nazis to testify because we need their help in the fight against neo-Nazis. However, what I did say and what I stand by to this day is that I see no sense in throwing a ninety-three-year-old man in prison. Such elderly perpetrators would not serve their sentence for very long, and most of them are already housebound anyway.

At the same time, these perpetrators can pay their dues in a much more valuable way—by confessing in public. I think it would be helpful for Germany and perhaps even for the survivors to see that the cooperation of such offenders has a purpose—to document everything that happened, especially for neo-Nazis and revisionists.

So it is not so much a question of whether these people should stand trial. Instead, I ask myself what happens to them when they stand trial as defendants. As far as I'm concerned, they can be found guilty, but part of their punishment should be to do community service by truthfully talking about the past in public. That would be of more use to Germany and the survivors.

That's why I continue to ask all the Democrats who are against the neo-Nazis, "What is the goal of our actions?"

If our goal is to punish, then all our efforts would still come up short. The punishments delivered are almost never hard enough, and the whole process doesn't bring about any good.

On the other hand, bearing witness to what happened has a far greater value than throwing an old man in jail. Incidentally, giving a sentence to a perpetrator, possibly a relatively mild sentence, doesn't really help survivors feel better. And it doesn't heal their wounds.

Nevertheless, my critics always reiterate that "we can only help the victims by throwing the perpetrators in jail."

I would like to see this played out once firsthand. How exactly would this help us, either me or the other survivors?

Again, I am not saying that we should let the perpetrators off the hook, but this puts all the focus on the offenders and none on the victims. And that's where I see a huge problem.

People also often criticize me for forgiving the Nazis. Why do the critics think I did it? Just because I wanted to be in the headlines?

Or was it because I stumbled onto an idea that helped me to process the past? It is an idea that freed me from my terrible past!

That alone would be a subject for worthwhile discussion with me. However, I don't really believe that my critics want to understand that. According to everything I've heard, many more survivors raise their voices to say, "It's all well and good that you want to forgive them, Eva, but why don't you do so within your own home? Why do you insist on doing it in public?"

That is their complaint. So I want to explain myself in a little more detail. Why do I forgive in public?

On one hand, it's because I want to explain to everyone how it all happened in the first place. I am not certain whether the survivors (and I mean *all* of them) truly understand that I didn't go to Auschwitz in 1995 with the former Nazi doctor Dr. Münch simply so that he could read my letter of forgiveness. No! It was so he could confirm the existence of the gas chambers!

I managed to organize a meeting with a Nazi, and he agreed to bear witness to the existence of the gas chambers and to describe the methods of the Nazis. My letter of forgiveness emerged in response to this, but my critics ignore this important point and treat it as if it never existed. But it is decisive! This step is extremely important for posterity—to meet a Nazi and have him confirm a document of this type. The critics should take this to heart. For a similar reason, I was also prepared to meet Oskar Gröning and shake his hand. I wanted to see what would happen and find out if this encounter could result in something positive.

At the same time (still to the question of why I made my act of forgiveness public), the moment I felt the power of forgiveness, I felt as if I had discovered a cure for cancer. It was unbelievable! Many people consider hate and anger to be pathogens for the soul, and I felt as if I had discovered a medicine to combat this proliferation of tumors. It made me happy, and I was not hurting anyone with it.

Should I keep all that to myself, or was I instead obliged to share my perspective with the rest of the world? It was not as if I had developed a new drug I wanted to sell. I have no financial advantage from my discovery—my deep conviction is and remains helping people. It is not about a business model.

And people from all over the world get in touch with me who specifically want my help.

Just a few weeks ago, I was in a school and a student approached me. She said that her parents beat her; she was crying and didn't know what to do. It breaks my heart again and again to see young people suffer. The girl had wide eyes, and these beautiful eyes were unbelievably sad. They touched my heart. I agreed to stay in contact with her in order to help her through this difficult time.

I told her that I had also hated my mother and father for many years. After Auschwitz I was left as an orphan. There was nowhere I belonged, no one loved me, no one made sure I had enough to eat and clothes to wear; I had to struggle in that situation.

But isn't it a thousand times easier today? In many respects, apparently it is not.

Life is still difficult for a young girl today. I know all too well what goes on in the head of a teenage girl. Would this girl be able to find someone who could help her if I didn't speak my thoughts in public? That's why it is urgently necessary to speak about forgiveness. And I think that the same is true in the Jewish community.

During the same school presentation, a woman later told me that her father is a survivor, but she knows absolutely nothing about him because he never wanted to talk about his experiences. And she was very sad about this. She needed to forgive her father because he had never talked with her. She felt as though he had excluded her. He had treated her less like a father and more like an office supervisor keeping her at arm's length. That's why there were no genuine conversations between them. Neither attention nor empathy.

I hear life stories like this nearly every week, from so many people that the accusation that I only tell my story for publicity is simply absurd. I am not concerned with publicity for myself; instead, I want to spread the idea that we no longer have to be victims and that we have the power to act to heal our wounds. By healing our wounds, we contribute to helping heal every cancerous growth that has spread in the hearts and souls of so many people.

That's why I wish that my critics would rather approach me personally instead of publicly discrediting me—to see if we can perhaps get along after all.

Maybe I would have turned out to be just like my critics if I had been ten years older in Auschwitz. Maybe I would have been just as overwhelmed by anger and thoughts of revenge since I would have understood what was happening in the world when I was in Auschwitz. But as a ten-year-old girl, I was not angry. It was my world.

One day my husband also told me that he knew exactly when D-Day started.

"How could you know?" I asked him gruffly. "I didn't know anything about what was going on in the world."

I was a child, barely old enough to survive.

However, Mickey was several years older and secretly listened to the news on a battery-powered radio with other prisoners in Latvia.

⊁ ⋆ ⊁

Perhaps Gröning was drawn to me because I approached him without intent; I was simply looking for information. In that respect, it was similar to my encounter with Dr. Münch. At that time I was also curious about him in order to obtain information.

Yet, I never would have believed that either of these men could also be interested in me.

Gröning even demonstrated a certain willingness to make a statement. It was difficult for him. He spoke about "incidents" when referring to the murder of many, many people. He did not use the word "murder." Even though there is no other word for what he described—a crying baby, left by its mother with her luggage, crying, incessantly crying, until an SS soldier grabbed the baby and hurled it against a truck. In that moment, his heart "stood still."

At the very least, he managed to make a striking statement at the end of the trial. Through his lawyer, Gröning declared that he would not ask the victims for forgiveness in court. Due to the vast scale of the suffering, this would not be possible for him. "I can only ask the Lord my God for forgiveness."

Many survivors have refused to acknowledge the value of his statement. They simply wanted to pillory him. But their rage doesn't help us survivors. The question is rather: Can we collectively learn from such processes? Does this further society?

Instead, making Nazis talk about their actions in public would be much more valuable than a prison sentence. Particularly for neo-Nazis who deny Auschwitz and all the war crimes. When I talk about Auschwitz as a victim, these neo-Nazis don't listen anyway. They say, "Oh, she's just a survivor, and that's why she's lying." But if someone like Gröning talked about Auschwitz, then the neo-Nazis couldn't simply go back to their business as usual.

I would have loved to ask Gröning something completely different: "Have you led a happy life?"

I'd also ask another major question: "What did you actually do after you finished your work in Auschwitz? How did you sleep at night? How did you function in the *machinery*?"

Because I suspect that Gröning didn't function perfectly at all—in contrast to the claims of his official statement. It is on record that he requested a transfer from Auschwitz several times, as did Dr. Münch. Both were no longer children when they entered Auschwitz; it was their free choice. Gröning even applied to go to the Russian front in order to leave Auschwitz, but his application was declined. I suspect that Rudolf Höss wanted to prevent eyewitness reports about everything that was going on in Auschwitz.

Yes, and I would have liked to ask Gröning one last personal question.

I have already mentioned that I was not hanged after I was caught stealing potatoes in Auschwitz. I was one of the Mengele twins, that is right, but I would like to hear from Gröning whether there was also an unwritten rule that the overseers could turn a blind eye when a survivor organized food in some way—in order to simply survive. That perhaps even the Nazis in Auschwitz respected it when someone put their life on the line in order to survive.

It bothers me since I received a letter from the daughter of a Holocaust survivor whose mother had also organized stealing potatoes. Now you have to know that cooking potatoes gives off a certain smell. In our barracks alone, there were twenty children preparing potatoes every night. Our overseers must have smelled that! Of course we only cooked them when everyone else was asleep, but the smell still couldn't be hidden.

However, we were not stopped a single time.

I know that Mengele hated it when someone begged for something. But if some of the children had found a way to survive by stealing potatoes, then is it possible that something like that would be silently tolerated?

I asked Gröning's lawyer for another meeting with him multiple times, alone, without the press. The response? He was too weak, so a meeting was probably out of the question.

So my questions will presumably remain unanswered.

I already know another answer: he was human despite everything. And he really liked me.

At the same time, he had no reason to like me. I forgave him, but I also told him he had to take responsibility for his actions.

By no means did I offer him a blank slate.

﹡ ﹡ ﹡

When dealing with such war criminals, who continue living among us for years after their crimes, countless moral questions arise.

The perpetrators cannot change what has happened; no one can do that. What's done is done. These people were involved. But if they feel guilty about it, should they come clean about it in public? Absolutely!

Should these people be prosecuted for their deeds or their involvement? Yes!

These testimonies play an important role for historical analysis and to prevent the activities of other neo-Nazis. You have to imagine that even today people who were involved in the National Socialist dictatorship continue to live undisturbed in Germany. They are elderly people. But they don't speak out. You also have to keep in mind that all the Germans who are between ninety and ninety-five years old experienced this time. But they (usually) do not speak out about it.

Again, I am not interested in throwing these old men and women in jail. To me, that seems to be a very rigid, very German approach. Lock them up in jail, let them serve their sentence! Done!

To me, it would be more important to record their memories, as an audio or film document, and play these in classrooms. These would have to be honest memories, that much is clear. But having them provide this basis for discussion with young people is the right approach to dealing with alleged perpetrators. In this type of discussion, voices can be louder, as far as I'm concerned.

I am someone who also approaches neo-Nazis and confronts them with their ideas. Usually I am just met with mocking babble, "You are a nobody, you are Jewish."

"What exactly makes you so superior?" I respond. "The simple fact that you are here in front of me and hate me? What have you accomplished in your life that makes you so intent on feeling superior to me? Is it the arbitrary color of your white skin? I don't want to offend you, but that doesn't make you particularly superior."

Neo-Nazis have nothing to show, that is my recurrent experience.

Do racist words contribute anything that can benefit the world?

No, no, and no!

Being white and fiddling with a weapon does not make a person particularly superior. Any idiot can do that.

I am not guilty of being born a Jew, but at the same time I cannot hate Germans for being born German. Nobody chooses the country they want to be born into.

Germans are bright, hard-working, and intelligent, and by and large, they are people with good hearts. Unfortunately, they just made a grave mistake in choosing Adolf Hitler to be their "Führer."

Likewise, Jews are also bright, intelligent, and hard-working, but for some obscure reason, we are spit upon for identifying as Jews. But it is not our fault.

I don't know how to convince the world to stop pointing a finger at us, but I can honestly say that I am no longer willing to be a "good victim."

I will continue to fight with everything I have to dispute anti-Semites and racists.

※ ※ ※

One of the problems in dealing with anti-Semitic prejudices is the silence. In the past decades, people have barely spoken with each other in a real way. On the surface, the German–Israeli dialogue seems harmonious, but feelings of shame and rage accumulate underneath. There are injuries that neither the Germans nor the Israelis talk about.

That's why more and more Germans speak out and say, "We don't want to hear any more about the past. Enough is enough." And we want to create a beautiful new world with this attitude? Although so much is simmering beneath the surface?

No, that's not the way it works. You have to lay your cards on the table—all of them. And then talk about them.

That is also true for every other partnership. When you don't reveal the unsaid discrepancies, at some point a giant problem monster can rear its head.

That's why honesty is one of the most important traits to me. If we observe a typical Nazi family, on the other hand, it is quickly apparent that they hardly talk about what really matters.

Unfortunately, my critics do not acknowledge my pursuit of honesty; instead, they deem my concept to be "improper." They say I cannot forgive something that was done not only to me but to millions of people. My critics say that no one has the right to forgive in the name of everyone who has died.

I am well aware that many survivors are angry. I understand that. That's why I only speak in my own name.

$\star \; \star \; \star$

Nevertheless, I feel sorry for every person who cannot forgive. "Forgiveness without restrictions?" my critics challenge. There must be criteria for forgiveness.

I can only respond that forgiveness does not mean we have to pardon the diabolical acts of the Nazis or other perpetrators, nor does it mean we give offenders amnesty or political asylum. You have to consider justice and forgiveness separately.

"Doesn't the perpetrator first have to acknowledge his deeds and then ask for forgiveness?" I hear this question again and again.

Yes, I respond, the perpetrator has to accept responsibility. But these are two different steps.

My critics argue that the point is to accomplish justice, and forgiveness plays a subordinate role. For the moment that a survivor forgives, his murdered family members turn over in their graves.

And as a little side blow to my person, they say that I cannot contest the fact that I grew up without parents. Therefore, I do not know what it means to be happy.

I respond by asking, "So it follows that a life without pain would impair the remembrance of those murdered?"

The concept of forgiveness has little or nothing at all to do with the perpetrators. Instead, it is exclusively concerned with victims' desire to be free from the pain that has been inflicted on them and that weighs them down. The concept of forgiveness, likewise, has nothing to do with a religious orientation. All people long to be free of pain and wounds from the past. If that were limited to just one religion, or to all of them, there would be people who couldn't accept such limits.

My critics say that forgiveness means that you no longer speak about an issue. No! Forgiveness does not mean forgetting. Forgiveness cannot lead to forgetting because nothing that someone has experienced can simply be forgotten. It is a part of one's personality. These things shape our lives, for better or worse.

I have one answer for everyone who accuses me of too easily forgetting all that the Nazis did to me and my family—I am one of the few survivors who has opened a private museum of remembrance. I give interviews about my time in Auschwitz, give talks about what happened in Auschwitz. I travel all over the world to talk about the crimes of the Nazis; how could anyone accuse me of forgetting?

Sometimes people who really want to forget, who try with all their might, are only able to do so by turning to drugs and alcohol. And even then, it is nearly impossible to escape this pain. It simply doesn't work!

I think it is important to use this pain. It's even part of what distinguishes us; that is where our suppressed reserves of strength lie dormant.

With every hurdle that arises in my life, I immediately think about how I managed to crawl over that filthy floor in Auschwitz for two weeks. With this image in my mind, I can withstand anything.

And every person who has survived a conflict-ridden time would agree with me that they use this time of crisis as a point of strength—as an anchor—to solve current problems.

It is about looking back at the moment of anger, of rage, but also drawing strength from it since you managed to escape the situation without lasting damage. And you can use this strength to overcome future conflicts.

That's why I also danced the hora on the selection ramp during my last visit to Auschwitz.

"Why are you doing that?" one visitor asked me, appalled.

"Why not?" I replied.

There was so much sadness in Auschwitz that I no longer want to feel today. On the selection ramp, the Nazis robbed me of my joy in life. They destroyed my family. So why can't I dance to regain some of my joy in life?

I also smiled in Auschwitz for the same reason, which no one else does. When I was standing in front of the famous photo of the freed Mengele children, a disgruntled visitor came up to me and hissed, "That's just not acceptable. You don't smile in Auschwitz."

THE POWER OF FORGIVENESS

I replied, "Young lady, I am the girl in this photo. And I paid the price. So please do not tell me what I can and cannot do!" Auschwitz is already gray and sad as it is.

⁑ ⁎ ⁑

However, I usually encounter a different type of reaction in Auschwitz, particularly when German students visit the camp. These encounters are not planned, but since I regularly guide a group of visitors through Auschwitz, sometimes other people mix with our group. Kiel, my managing director, sometimes lets me know when a group of German students strolls past. And during our last visit, he even asked me to say a few spontaneous words.

So I turned to the group and said, "My name is Eva Kor, I am a survivor of Auschwitz."

The moment I said I was an Auschwitz survivor, all the German women began to wail and cry. So I asked, "What's wrong, do I look that awful?"

I tried to joke around a little since the situation had spiraled out of control. All of a sudden, for these students, everything that had happened in this place was no longer part of the chilling past, but of a specific life.

Then I said, "Do me a favor—don't feel guilty for what Germany has done. Guilt doesn't help anyone. Your only responsibility today and tomorrow is to speak out when you see something unjust. But what happened in the Second World War, which you weren't involved with, you don't need to worry about that. That is just a waste of energy. If you want to do something in remembrance of the people who were killed by the Nazis, go to the hospital once a month and spend an hour with a person who doesn't receive any visitors. Do some good. Develop positive projects. But guilt has never brought about change."

Doing good is always better than sitting in the corner and feeling guilty. That is called self-pity. And it is terrible.

I realize again and again that particularly young Germans carry around a huge burden with Hitler's legacy. They often ask me how I am able to forgive. And I always respond by saying that as young people, they have done nothing wrong. Why shouldn't I like them? They are innocent! If I were to judge them because Hitler did something terrible, then I would be catering to prejudices.

We can only judge people by their actions. I would even go as far as to say that the greatest tragedy for Germany is that Hitler has been dead for over seventy years. Because his burden still weighs down on the shoulders of the youngest generation.

None of us can choose where or into what conditions we are born. Children and grandchildren of survivors enjoy a great deal of support, while the children and grandchildren of camp overseers often do not. But these German children are also incredibly traumatized and receive no one's sympathy.

The children of survivors likewise have myriad problems. They have no grandparents and still ask about them constantly. "Joey has a grandmother, why don't I?"

When my daughter was three years old, we took a vacation with family friends. When I was cooking one evening, I held her in one arm and her gaze fell on my tattoo. Her friend's mother didn't have such a tattoo. That troubled my daughter, and at some point she asked the woman, "Where is your number, actually?"

Afterward, my daughter came back to me and said, "Mommy! That woman has no number. Why doesn't she have a number?"

I told her, "You remember the mean people who killed your grandparents? The same people put this number on my arm."

I answered every one of these questions. I talked with my kids because my parents had tried to spare us. They told us that Hitler wouldn't come; but instead, we were taken to him. I wished they had told us the truth since I had no idea about what could happen. I was not reassured. The reality was too close and too real for me to ignore it.

That's why I swore to myself that if I ever had kids of my own, I would always answer their questions truthfully. It is a mistake to try to protect kids from the "seriousness of life," since when the fun is over, it's usually too late.

Today, Germany can be proud of itself. It is the only country in the world that has taken responsibility for the deeds of its grandparents and great-grandparents by offering reparations. No other country in Europe has done so to a comparable degree. When the conversation turns to the past, everyone points their finger at Germany.

But at the same time, other countries were also allied with Hitler's Germany. That is an issue that is addressed far too rarely. There were many countries involved in the Holocaust. But every single one of these countries simply points the finger at Germany and renounces all of its own guilt. As if none of them had ever done any wrong. Come on!

I know from my own experience that the Hungarian Nazis were brutal. They were the ones who burned my father's fingernails because they wanted to know where he had hidden his gold. It wasn't the Germans.

And my husband was born in Latvia, where the Riga ghetto was known as one of the most violent in the whole empire. Germany had never operated it. The ghetto was in the hands of Latvians, who terrorized the Jews there and finally murdered most of all the Latvian Jews.

I know that many Poles also distance themselves from Auschwitz. They say it was a German camp and they have nothing to do with it. But it isn't that simple. Anti-Semitism is not a problem that only concerns Germany. Many countries have a responsibility for their own part in the blame.

On the other hand, Germany is the only country I know of that openly and intentionally assumes its share of responsibility for its diabolical acts. That is the most that Germany can do as a country—offer compensation.

If I received restitution from Hungary or my husband received it from Latvia, I would be pleased. But these countries have not even considered it. They say, "No, we have done nothing wrong."

These countries do not even want to think about this kind of compensation. Nazi Germany was the instigator of all the suffering, that is true; Germany was the country where it all began, but it would be wrong to simply point the finger at Germany and wash one's own hands of the matter.

In Germany today, the country has accepted responsibility for its actions. No one else has done that. It wasn't the German troops who stormed into our house to deport us. It was the Hungarians.

Meanwhile, in Austria and Italy, the idea prevails among many people that their parents and grandparents were first and foremost victims of the Nazi regime. However, the facts tell a different story. I can only appeal to those young people to take the responsibility of history seriously—whatever happened in those volatile times, for better or worse, down to the present. You are a part of your country, and your country's history is yours as well.

I have also never considered having my tattoo removed. Never! This thought never bothered me. Sometimes people are amazed by this. I am even proud of my tattoo (with the exception of my paranoid reaction in Vienna when I covered my arms).

When people ask me about the numbers on my skin today, I answer (without any trace of emotion) that I was in Auschwitz, where I was given this tattoo. People often then ask if I would like to have it removed, and I always respond by saying, "If I remove my tattoo, would the entire tragedy I was put through also vanish?"

Unfortunately, the answer is no. So why should I subject myself to additional pain?

It is like a medal of bravery. I like to look at it, even though it isn't written clearly. That's okay—after all, I know why the numbers are so blurry.

However, I am not a fan of the tattoos for fashion nowadays. One young woman explained to me, "I do it because I want to be unique."

In my eyes, she may have a crazy tattoo now, but that doesn't make her unique. Uniqueness does not come from people changing their external appearance or from their choice in clothing.

The type of uniqueness that radiates into the world comes from how you conduct yourself in the world. Inner strength is essential. A little color on your skin doesn't change who you are inside. And isn't that the only part of you that truly matters?

Sometimes I tell young people, "Let me offer you a business deal. I will give you the most valuable diamond in the world, and in return, you give me your heart, mind, and soul."

Sadly, quite a few actually choose the diamond. I explain to them that the diamond that sparkles in me cannot be bought for any sum of money in the world. Because I feel good about the way that I am, and the things I do. And I feel good when I try to treat other people with respect.

Many young people are insecure. They are testing out how to find their place in this complex world. I would advise them to do something they are proud of. Start something that gives you inner strength. Every person can be valuable, and it doesn't take a bunch of money to do so.

One way to do so could be to read more. That opens your mind to unexpected worlds, to knowledge about humanity. And it forms your character.

Or you can learn to help others, even with the smallest gestures. Or if you suffer from bad habits, the first step should be to change these habits. This type of change develops a strong personality.

Forgiveness is also a personal change and an active step. We mustn't wait for an apology to happen first—although we are all waiting for that, sometimes for years, sometimes for our whole lives.

However, it is a bad idea to wait for an apology.

I recall an encounter I had with a Jewish Holocaust expert at a conference. Although I had never seen him or spoken to him before, he approached me and gave me a kiss. So I was a little reserved. Apparently some people like to kiss me—I don't know why.

At some point I said to him, "You must like my idea of forgiveness . . ."

"No," he answered. "Quite the contrary. You have to understand that in the Jewish tradition, the perpetrators have to come crawling on their hands and knees and plead for forgiveness."

"Okay," I responded. "Let's look at that more closely. If Rudolf Höss Himmler, Mengele, Hitler, and Göring were still alive today, do you really think they would come crawling and plead to us for forgiveness?"

"That is absurd."

"Does that mean that by the same token, I am not allowed to forgive? That I have to remain their victim for the rest of my life?"

He didn't answer.

But that is the crucial point. According to this logic, the Nazi leaders still determine that I am a victim, even decades after their deaths. Which means I would allow these people to have a say in my life. That is crazy!

"Then I would be dependent on these perpetrators all over again," I argued. "Me, the victim, dependent on the mercy of the perpetrator? That's what I call absurd!"

That's why I am so insistent on forgiveness. Because I determine that I want to be free. I don't need a Nazi to condescend to me and ask for forgiveness.

⁎ ⁎ ⁎

"Simon Wiesenthal didn't forgive either."

This is an argument I have heard multiple times. On one hand, I answer that if Wiesenthal couldn't forgive, then he remained a spiritual prisoner. On the other hand, it wasn't possible because that's exactly what people expected from him.

You cannot forgive simply because other people think it is a nice idea. You forgive because you realize that's the way to become strong and to free yourself. There is no ceremony, no magic formula necessary; it is only significant for the victim.

When I forgive the Nazis, it encompasses every wound, every injury. My view of forgiveness is better than the handed-down tradition that waits for someone to come crawling for forgiveness.

When we don't forgive, we remain in chains. We are chained to the perpetrators as well as the past.

Several years ago, I visited a few members of the German Bundestag. Thinking I could give them some good advice, I suggested that Germany should forgive the Nazis and Hitler because that would help Germany heal an open wound. One of the politicians politely told me, "Well, Ms. Kor, that is very nice. But what would the neo-Nazis think if we were to forgive the Nazis? We feel them breathing down our necks. They create many problems for us. And as a member of the parliament, I must tell you that it's my responsibility to protect the citizens of this country. And your suggestion does not really help us protect our citizens."

I responded, "You are right."

In this case, I had to admit that I hadn't thought the matter through properly. At this point I had assumed that governments could forgive. But in this discussion, I realized how important it was to protect a country's citizens. A government cannot simply forgive with a blank check since that would put the country in an awfully dangerous position. A government is likewise unable to forgive at the request of an individual.

The truth is that I cannot forgive for someone else, I can only forgive for myself. So every single person who has been injured or broken—everyone who carries the burden of various atrocities—must forgive in his or her own name.

Every single individual has to reconcile and forgive in their heart.

That's also why no single person can forgive in the name of all the Holocaust survivors. You are likewise unable to forgive someone for something he or she did to someone else. It is a very personal act.

Yet the act of forgiveness also sets an example.

For instance, we should all be role models for our children by refusing to get wrapped up in vengeful thinking. Or as President Abraham Lincoln once said, "Do I not destroy my enemies when I make them my friends?"

That's why I always taught my kids this message: You don't have to fight my battles, for there are no battlefields anymore.

There is a framed quote by Edmund Burke in the entryway of the museum that says, "All that is necessary for the triumph of evil is that good men do nothing."

It carries particular significance since an arson attack was carried out on my Holocaust museum in 2003. The attacker was never found. There were several suspects but conclusive evidence was lacking.

It was a very difficult time. You have to imagine that we had just purchased the entire building. My business partner in the travel agency that shared the building had declared bankruptcy after 9/11. People's desire to go on long-distance journeys had suddenly dissipated in the wake of Bin Laden's attacks. We had no sponsors, and there was no public funding. So I took a risk and bought the entire building on my own. I took sole responsibility for all the costs that accrued, as a private person, with a private loan.

And all of a sudden the house was in flames.

I drove there immediately and stood next to the fire engine while the flames flickered through the roof and ate their way through the building. They burned everything down to the foundation walls. Two reporters had already made their way to the building and pushed a microphone into my face. It was midnight. And they asked me, "How do you feel?"

"There have been better days in my life," I answered quietly.

"What will you do now?"

"I have no doubt that I will rebuild this building," I said. "Even if it costs me every last penny. I won't let evil triumph."

That's precisely what would have let the attacker triumph— my giving up. My defeat.

I never imagined that the news would reach the national press—it even appeared in the *New York Times*, whose reporting had a domino effect and led to hundreds of thousands of dollars in donations pouring in within three months. We had never before put out such a call for donations. It was unbelievable! You have to imagine that all the schools in the area participated in the call to action. There were elementary school kids collecting donations on their lunch breaks. I opened all the checks in a festive ceremony and saw these enthusiastic, sweet students.

I asked a six-year-old, "What do you know about this museum?"

He answered, "I know that when you were my age, there were a lot of people who were very mean and wanted to kill you. And that was wrong."

The kids had grasped the essential message, and their teacher had done a good job. In our area, the elementary school kids alone collected over $1,000 with raffles.

That's how our museum was rebuilt. It took one year of construction, one year of heartache. But I felt better each day.

However, of course the mortgage still had to be paid. And after the fire, the fire insurance refused to renew our policy. It was obvious that no other insurance would take us on. On the other hand, it was impossible to reopen the museum without fire insurance. I had to use my powers of persuasion to convince them. I even asked the state governor for his help by asking if there is a law against terminating a client's policy in the case of a fire. And somehow I managed to secure a renewal.

At the same time, the costs were getting out of hand. We are not a public institution, but a private museum. Our monthly costs were around $2,000 for the gutted building.

In short, it was not an easy time.

And I was supposed to forgive the attacker for all of that?

It wasn't easy.

As I mentioned, the financial hardship was astronomical, but I had decided to no longer harbor hatred.

＊ ＊ ＊

The time will come, I thought to myself, *when I can easily find it in myself to forgive. Because I can recognize that deep down, the person who did such a thing is a deeply sick person. And I cannot change them.* Ever since, I have asked myself again and again: Why would someone want to do that to me?

At first there was shock, then disbelief and finally, I wondered, do I hate this person?

It was clear to me that if this situation in fact caused me to be overcome by hatred and anger, then I would be a victim once again. While the flames were still shooting out of the building, I could feel how easy it was to fall back into the victim mentality.

Indeed, I told everyone that I was sad about what had happened. And yes, I truly was. But I didn't want to let the flames rule me.

A couple years ago, an incident led several trusted friends to suggest that I needed police protection around the clock—when I was at home, in the museum, even when I went out shopping. After one month—and associated costs of around $20,000—I told Kiel, my managing director, that I would end the police protection. Except in the museum, for the simple reason of ensuring safety for visitors and employees, but I no longer wanted police protection for my house or my daily life.

If there was really a crazy person walking around out there who had set his mind on shooting me, then he would find a way to do so. No sheriff could stop him.

I am not afraid.

If I am honest, my biggest fear is of falling and hitting my head while cleaning house. I worry more about that than about a crazy person rushing up to shoot me.

☆ ☆ ☆

Forgiveness has to be put into practice. It has to become a lifestyle.

It is not enough to just read about it.

You have to inhale forgiveness, you have to soak it up. It's like when you set a goal to lose a few pounds through exercise. If you just buy a video in which the trainer gives instructions, but you aren't prepared to get off the couch and thrust your arms and legs into the air, it will have no effect. It's not about reading the right books and videos; you also have to practice your chosen method.

Forgiveness must become your own path. It has to become part of your personality.

Perhaps the reality looks a little different than in the video (to stick to the example of exercise), but forgiveness needs to become part of your daily life.

Only then will you be able to eliminate anger and annoyance from your everyday life. And only then will you feel its tremendous power. It's like an energy source you can tap into at any time, whenever you want or need it. Forgiveness wields so much power that in the end you won't want to give it up.

A few days ago, a child asked me in my Holocaust museum, "How many years does it take to really forgive?" I had to smile because there are no standards for forgiveness.

Depending on the severity of the circumstances, it can often take years for the flood of emotions to subside. But it shouldn't take fifty years, the way it did in my case. If you have become more familiar in dealing with your pain and have understood the power you have at your disposal to transform your entire life, then you will learn forgiveness very quickly.

Every day that you devote to your anger is another day that your tormenter is still in control of you.

You already hold the key to your freedom.

Therefore, forgive. It will heal you.

6

How Forgiveness Can
Change the World

How do we want to shape the future?

Should we really limit ourselves to pointing the finger at each other?

No!

However, when I decide to make friends with Germans, I have to be prepared to treat them like my other friends. When something bothers me, I need to be able to tell them. And by the same token, I also expect my German friends to tell me when something about me bothers them. After all, without mutual honesty, we won't be able to solve any problems.

But first of all, we have to be honest with ourselves.

We cannot simply long for paradise and talk ceaselessly about how nice and easy everything is, while in truth we are only suppressing our dissatisfaction. That doesn't help the world a single bit. When anger and hate continue to boil over in us then that is the perfect breeding ground for war.

On the other hand, forgiveness is the seed for freedom. And it heals trauma and tragedies. Forgiveness is the only means to free yourself and achieve true independence.

I am often reminded of Viktor Frankl. Particularly when I am suddenly overwhelmed by feelings of distress myself.

Viktor Frankl, who lived from 1905 to 1997, was an Austrian neurologist and psychiatrist who was deported to the ghetto of Theresienstadt with his wife and parents in 1942. His father died there, and his mother and brother were murdered in the gas chambers of Auschwitz. His wife died in Bergen-Belsen. Frankl, on the other hand, was deported to Auschwitz in 1944 and later sent to a satellite camp of the concentration camp Dachau, where he was freed by the American army in 1945.

After the war, he documented his experiences in the book *Man's Search for Meaning*. As the founder of logotherapy and existential analysis, he mainly wrote about the hidden meaning of affliction and founded a philosophical school of thought devoted to it. He often gives accounts of people so weighed down by their fate that it seems they cannot go on.

Until it passes and they manage to go on after all.

Hitting rock bottom in this way can lead to very deep insights on life. In fact, it's always when we are no longer able to change a situation that we are challenged to change ourselves.

Dr. Frankl was always a great role model for me when it came to finding something positive in a hopeless situation. One good example is an eighty-three-year-old man who attended one of

Frankl's presentations. He was inconsolable about his wife having died the year before.

He is unable to deal with her death and struggles with suicidal thoughts, and Viktor Frankl asks him in a seemingly offhand way, "What would have happened if you had died first?"

The man answers, "Oh, that would have been terrible. I don't think that my wife would have been able to cope with it. I am glad that *she* doesn't have to go through this. . . ."

As he is speaking, he suddenly realizes that he saved his wife from the blow of having to go on without *him*. All of a sudden, his suffering takes on new meaning. On a higher level. As harsh as it may sound, there is some kind of hidden *meaning* in suffering. That's exactly why this psychologist's work is so incredibly interesting to me.

Frankl's work has enabled me to understand that if I forgive, then I'll even forgive when no one else understands since I will in fact live on a higher level of consciousness. In the beginning, that was by no means my goal (and I do not want to write a step-by-step guide here about how to attain this "higher level of consciousness"), but I have grasped that, as Frankl writes:

"Only under the hammer blows of fate, in the white heat of suffering, does life take on form and shape."

I have experienced it and accepted it. And with this realization, it doesn't take any more effort to finally forgive those who kindled this "white heat of suffering" to begin with.

For Frankl, one trigger was a call from one of his students who had been in a bad accident.

"Are you doing okay?" Frankl asked him with concern.

"I've never been better," the student answered. "I have never been happier."

This student became 100 percent paralyzed because he jumped into a swimming pool with no water. Paralyzed from the neck down.

Dr. Frankl asked him, "How is that possible?"

"You know," the student replied, "now I can dedicate my entire life to people who are suffering from a ton of psychological problems. I have nothing else to do besides this one thing, and that makes me very happy. I've found my calling."

Viktor Frankl was speechless. What goes on inside people when they are forced to write off all their physical abilities and completely rely on their mental and spiritual capacities? How can someone be happy who cannot wiggle a foot or wave a hand?

This is precisely the point at which Frankl posits the higher meaning in human existence.

Of course, I don't know if this applies to everyone.

But I have seen people who were born without legs and still became athletes. And they seem to be happy. That's why I ask myself whether being happy and being fortunate are directly connected. Most likely they aren't because at the same time we see people who seem to be perfect on the outside—they look perfect and healthy, have a high social status, and no financial problems—but they aren't happy.

So how does happiness come about?

Now, if you dedicate your life to things that are meaningful, then you aren't off to such a bad start.

If you are unhappy today, even though you earn enough money and are surrounded by loving friends and family, then the root of your sadness is in yourself. You will not find happiness as long as you concentrate more on what other people have than on yourself. Incidentally, this is not to be confused with egotism. Quite the contrary. The same is true of habits such as constantly buying new clothes, enjoying the best food, driving the nicest car, or owning a bigger house. None of that has ever made people happy. There are simply too many millionaires who have given up on life. Only when you dedicate your life to something that's greater than you will you find meaning in life and thus happiness—and that is exactly what the paraplegic student is doing by helping other people with their comparatively moderate problems.

As Frankl writes so aptly, "Those who have a *why* to live, can bear with almost any *how*."

He supposedly adopted this concept from Nietzsche, but it is still incomparably true. As long as I know why I suffer, I can overcome any crisis. That's why a mother can overcome any difficulty in order to protect her children. She can get through anything because she knows for whom she is overcoming obstacles and passing through low points.

On the other hand, it is very difficult to start the day with no motivation.

It is still not necessarily beneficial to look for meaning when you're right in the middle of a mess. And if someone is pointing a gun at you, something like *forgiveness* suddenly becomes very trivial anyway.

Your first task should always be to secure a safe environment. And then to live in complete safety and freedom before you can develop a deeper understanding of life's questions. Because people's primary instinct is always the survival instinct.

I saw people in Auschwitz try everything imaginable in order to survive. Every day. Of course there were also people who lost all the courage to face life, but they were a small minority.

⋆ ⋆ ⋆

How do we want to shape the future?

After all, forgiveness can change the world.

It starts small, but little by little, forgiveness can transform a city, a country, the world. I firmly believe that everything good in the world starts with a single person (as does everything bad). And even an inconspicuous person—maybe you—can lead the way.

I see the children at the foundation of all this. There is still time to plant a seed in them. Children are still receptive to ideas for the good of the world. First they are selfish, because every child wants to be the smartest, the strongest, the most beautiful, maybe even the best dressed. That's why I would immediately spread the following saying in the schools, "You are not better than your schoolmate." School uniforms may even be constructive in this respect.

It is important that as soon as a child is called a mocking nickname, we respond immediately so that even the youngest can be taught forgiveness. For ridicule and scorn change the atmosphere and cannot be taken back. I would hope for decisive intervention when it comes to insults and taunts—from kindergarten to elementary school to high school and in all further education. Can you imagine how drastically people's cooperation with one another would improve if all of a country's citizens learned to forgive each other (and themselves) from the time they were little?

Even when these people encounter the blows of life, they do not give up. Instead, they experience something similar to riding a bicycle. If you have ever learned how to sit on the seat and pedal while keeping your balance, you will never forget it for the rest of your life.

From an early age, our children would have the self-assurance necessary to come to grips with any affliction. And they would grow up with a sense of authentic, wise self-confidence.

For forgiveness has never made someone else a victim.

I forgive you—I do not hurt you.

In order to teach such a simple but revolutionary lesson in the schools, even an hour each semester would make a difference. Discussing a film or a quote from a book would be enough. But it all depends on an individual person being willing to teach forgiveness.

One evening, at an award ceremony, I encountered an older woman who was constantly smiling from ear to ear.

"May I sit next to you?" she asked me.

"Of course."

We started to talk, and the topic of forgiveness came up. Then this stranger told me, "That's what I like about you. You have an aura about you that I have rarely seen in people."

"You don't know me!"

"No, I've never seen you before, but I like the expression in your eyes. There's something hidden there that made me feel obliged to speak with you."

As it turned out, she was a widely known TV reporter who was so enamored with my statements about forgiveness that she absolutely wanted to get her hands on something to take home and study on her own time. Her husband had left her for a younger woman, and she hated him for it—so much so that she was no longer in control of herself. At home I recorded some of my thoughts on a cassette for her. I sent it to her, and she forgave her husband.

"I feel sorry for him," she wrote me a few weeks later. "In the meantime, he looks like an old fool. I don't even know what I saw in him when I married him. But that was a long time ago."

Later she passed around the cassette in her circle of friends. What these people like about my concept is that they don't have to climb Mount Everest to attain results. Every person can listen to my thoughts at home or even at work and meditate on them.

On her own initiative, this woman got the ball rolling. That's the point.

I wish there were also more programs for drug addicts and alcoholics who are likewise running away from a hole in their soul. But there is no escape from the chaos in one's own heart.

Despite my catastrophic, devastated childhood, I never felt the need to take drugs or drink alcohol. It's much more important to me that my brain is unimpaired and that I can use it freely. I would rather have a clear state of mind. That's why it's incomprehensible to me that so many people would rather flee from themselves their whole life long.

Countless people feel that they have been unfairly accused, possibly even unjustly thrown in jail. That may be true; but with what kind of expectations do these victims of the justice system torture themselves?

Do they really expect the police responsible to eat humble pie before them and leaders to step down? Everything is possible, but it seems to me that many people are waiting in vain.

That's why I would like to urge these people—even those who have perhaps spent many years sitting in a dirty prison cell—to forgive all the police officers and judges. And to admit that they made mistakes.

I would advise victims: Realize that no one can change what has happened, and stop wasting your time and energy on these distractions.

Sometimes people misunderstand this point. I am not concerned with just sitting down and forgiving a little. The whole point is to take back *power* over your own life.

What does that mean?

It means that when someone does something terrible to you, by forgiving them, you can regain the power to move on. So that what occurred doesn't ruin your day. Or, in the worst case, your whole life. This realization offers incredible strength.

If we would only consider how many military disputes started because something "wrong" was done at some point, which has been avenged ever since. Supposedly. In turn, the other side also has to get revenge. Supposedly. And in turn, the first side fires up their bombers again.

Putting an end to this vicious cycle of violence, because it is not necessary, means *creating peace*.

Forgiveness is not a strategy for countering a violent outbreak. Forgiveness is no guarantee of safety in acute danger. For when we realize that our lives are in danger, then most people will try to do anything imaginable in order to save their lives. But forgiveness is something that comes into effect after the trauma has occurred.

There is no reason for all this suffering. For all the pain. For all the anger.

In their place: *peace.* And the freedom to establish one's own life.

Instead of building air-raid shelters and rocket launchers, let's build the foundations for new schools.

Now you can say that this attitude is an incredibly simplified view of the world, maybe even naive—I hear it all the time. I can only say that I would rather be naive than angry. I'd especially rather be naive than so angry that I can no longer see any hope in the world.

I do not want to live on a planet where hope cannot grow. Especially not among people who are uninterested in working to shape a better tomorrow than today.

Some time ago, a car with four visitors stopped in front of our museum. As they were leaving, they seemed fearful, worried, and not necessarily happy. I went out to them and said, "You can't do that here. You can learn all about the atrocities and what happened, but when you go back outside, I want to see a smile on your faces and hope in your hearts."

After all, I live in the same world as other people do. I see snow in the winter, I feel heat in summer. And when my feet sink down into the snow in winter, I know that in twenty-five or thirty days, spring will once again take hold. So I behold the gray winter day and say to myself, "Okay, we are one day closer to spring."

I shared these thoughts with that group of visitors, and then they smiled after all and hugged me. I like that. When I am able to make people happy, I am all the more happy myself.

If we just concentrate on life's tragedies and how sad we feel, then I wonder how other people come to believe that hope leads to despair. Again and again, inevitably, there will be another sunrise, even after the greatest disaster.

Can you imagine what would happen if every victim worldwide were to forgive?

Happy people do not long for war. That's why I emphasize again and again that anger is the seed of war. On the other hand, forgiveness is the seed of peace.

⋟ ⋆ ⋟

After I visited Auschwitz with Dr. Münch in 1995, a German journalist wrote an article about it. In our preliminary talk, I thought he wanted to write about forgiveness, but instead he outed Dr. Münch as an entrenched old Nazi, complete with his address. After that, his house was attacked by arsonists three times. I was appalled. It was my fault that this ninety-three-year-old man's house was in flames three times. He did not really understand what was happening since he suffered from dementia.

I contacted the journalist and asked him what he had been thinking. He answered, "I settled the score for my grandfather, a survivor of Auschwitz."

Is that so?

In my view of the situation, Dr. Münch did something important. He traveled to Auschwitz with me and signed an eyewitness testimony about the terrible atrocities committed in the camp. And how was he rewarded? With arson attacks.

Will the vicious cycle of revenge ever end?

Anger is a seed of war.

That's why I count on people who support me and long for *peace*. All around the world.

Neo-Nazis are likewise full of anger. They see themselves as superhuman—not because they are crazy, but on the contrary, because they were raised with and taught to hate from an early age.

The problem is that we have all forgotten how to recognize when we are stuck in a hateful environment. All that neo-Nazis even dimly perceive is that their pain is caused by someone else— from either their own government or another government, from the Americans, the Jews, the blacks, the immigrants, or someone else. And this blaming warps their minds. The energy they waste by doing so is unequaled since the act of hating takes a higher toll on the body than loving does.

Why do people even join these groups, which are guided by hate in the first place? They could use their time to get an education, and they could initiate something positive. Instead, they waste it on hate. It's easy to understand why, when you consider that the immediate environment in which they are growing up is filled with hate. And hate is the "Lord's Prayer" of all Nazis.

These people are not mentally ill. They were simply taught to hate instead of to love.

That is why I sometimes worry about what is going on in the world. Will there be another Auschwitz? A new Rwanda? A new Darfur? Our blue planet has obviously not learned its lesson yet. Where will the next genocide take place?

Maybe an international peace conference should be held on the selection ramp in Auschwitz in order to clearly demonstrate to participants what actually happens when we don't resolve our problems.

There is one relatively simple way to stop neo-Nazis: get up and vote! In the US, the voter turnout is low. Forty percent of voters in the US are not interested in what is going on. But how can we expect democracy in any other way? Interestingly, the antidemocrats are more strongly represented in these "votes of the minority" because their supporters enthusiastically take advantage of their democratic right to vote.

I can only appeal to every individual person to go and vote if you want to prevent another Auschwitz. If you want to prevent another genocide—go vote!

Choose a candidate who is familiar with economic questions and has experience in dealing with the economy since when the economy doesn't work, people look for scapegoats. But this candidate should also express opposition to terrorism and advocate for human rights.

As I said, if you don't go to vote, then you are voting for the neo-Nazis and terrorists. That needs to be clear to every one of us.

Two years ago, I was in Romania with a group of about sixty people, and I visited Portz, my little hometown. We took part in a ceremony with the mayor and then cemented six memorial walkway plaques in place. Every resident who strolls past the place my family once lived from now on will encounter these plaques and, with them, the life stories of deported Jews.

The village community welcomed me with open arms. One young man even stood up and said in Romanian, "We are so proud of you. You are one of us."

That deeply moved me. I had to think of my parents. And that's why I would like to include a portrait of them here.

⸷ ⋆ ⋆

My mother: Jaffa Mozes

When she married my father, people told her she would have a good life. But she did not like life as a farmer and was never truly happy in Portz. Life there was too monotonous for her, and she had to work too hard.

I remember that my parents had frequent differences of opinion. Soon after the wedding, my mother threatened to leave my father and file for divorce. As a little kid, I didn't understand what all of that meant. However, I did understand that my mother was very unhappy. It seemed to me that her life was exactly the same from week to week and year to year.

It was as if all she ever did was feed the animals, wash clothing, do the housework, or cook meals. In addition, my mother was unswervingly willing to cook for other people or to help a neighbor in need. I hardly ever saw her resting. But sometimes, on winter evenings, she loved to disappear into the bedroom to read or to spend time simply listening to music on the radio.

Every stranger who passed through our village and needed a place to sleep ended up at our house. There was no hotel or boarding house in our town, and the inn didn't offer any beds. So every traveler was sent to our home. No matter who knocked at our door, my mother welcomed each person. If the person was dirty, my mother and the maid (when she was there) spared no effort to make sure he took a warm bath and that his clothes were washed and cleansed of fleas. After the limitations imposed on the Jews from 1942 onward, my mother carried out all of these tasks alone.

Every villager who had a problem or needed advice naturally came to my mother. Among other reasons, they came to her because she was extremely well educated and understanding. And she endeavored to give advice as diligently as she carried out all her other tasks.

Monday was always laundry day. Since there were no washing machines in those days, the work was done in the nearby river. We went to the riverbank and beat every piece of laundry against the rocks there. Before they were boiled in a big kettle, we had to dunk them all in water. My mother also made her own soap. In winter, everything followed the same procedure, but we did laundry less often. The winter clothes were usually made of wool, and I am sure that they must have been cleaned during one of the weekly trips to the city.

Thursday was always baking day. On Wednesday evenings, we filled pots with yeast dough. The pots were shaped like little baskets and made of wood We bought them regularly from the gypsies who passed through the village. My sisters and I helped my mother prepare the dough on Wednesday evening. We kneaded the dough in the containers so it could rise overnight. Mother had two or three containers that she used ceaselessly: one for the white challah bread, a braided bread for holidays; one for weekday bread; and one for cake. We always baked for the coming week.

After Mother had shaped the bread or cake, she used a long metal spatula to push the loaves deep into the oven. You could put quite a lot into that oven; my mother usually baked ten loaves of bread and three cakes at the same time.

She received help from the numerous relatives who were always visiting us. Even after 1943, relatives from the surrounding towns still continued to visit us. They stayed for a week or more. My mother cooked and baked extra portions for all of them and made sure that they all packed enough food for the trip home.

One of the aunts who visited us regularly was Aunt Irena; she was also the relative with whom we lived after the war. She was married to a lawyer and lived in comfort in Cluj, Hungary. The two of them usually visited us in a car driven by their chauffeur. They used to spend their holidays on the Riviera or in Paris or Rome.

I can recall another aunt who was married to a factory owner and lived in Bucharest. She was also very well-to-do and visited us regularly. Another one of my father's sisters lived in Kraszna, not very far from us, and we saw her regularly because she often lacked food or needed some type of help.

My mother was like an angel. She always had time for us. She took us shopping, or she read stories aloud to us. She loved to sing and shared this passion with us. When she was ironing, she sang songs, to our delight. We sang songs ceaselessly when we drove around in the carriage.

I have no idea how my mother managed to make all of her appointments since we had no telephone. Her appointments in the shops also worked out without any means of communication. For example, the cloth for our clothing, which was specially sent from a larger town, was stored in the bigger town of Széplak. Somehow we were notified that the material had arrived, and presto, my mother got us ready, took her best horse, summoned a driver and carriage, and lifted us onto the coach. Later, when we were forbidden to hire a driver, our father drove us.

When we entered the shop, the shopkeeper showed us magnificent magazines with the newest fashion trends. Our eyes nearly popped out of our heads. Of course my mother had the final say about our clothes, but I loved to flip through the magazines. It opened up an entirely new world to me.

Mother always wanted to have two identical outfits for the older girls, and two identical outfits for us two younger girls. She liked navy blue, white, and pink for Edit and Aliz and preferred wine-red, powder blue, white, and pink for Miriam and me. Once my mother had chosen the material and pattern, our measurements were taken, and another appointment was made for the fitting.

In this way, we each received six dresses a year. They must have cost a fortune. We occasionally received hand-me-downs from Edit and Aliz, but due to the four-year age difference, the older girls' clothes were a little too old-fashioned and mature for us. And since one of my elder sisters was a little larger than the other, the dresses had to be altered accordingly. In any case, it was thanks to these similarly designed dresses that Miriam and I were able to survive.

For her era, my mother was very well educated. That's why she was so concerned that her children also receive a substantial education. However, back then in Portz, the school only had four grades. My mother got my father to agree to have the girls go to high school and then even college. Which did not sit well with him.

I remember that my father had set his mind to it that my two older sisters would stop their education long before getting a high school diploma. He argued that they wouldn't need any further education because they would be married soon, after all. Moreover, he was convinced that too much education could get in the way of one's piety.

"My children will receive a good education," my mother countered relentlessly. "There is more to be read than just the prayer book. My girls will become educated women."

"I agree with you," my father finally relented, "but they must study at home. We will look for a tutor to live with us and prepare Edit and Aliz for the exam in high school. That way, they will only have to spend a few days in the city."

My mother agreed to the compromise. This is how a *Fräulein* came into our lives. She spoke German, and along with the German language, she taught the girls music, drawing, and history. In addition, she lived with us. At some point in early 1944, the Fräulein stopped coming. We heard that she was deported along with the other German Jews.

I don't know what ever happened to her. Maybe she survived. Maybe she fared better than my mother did—this amazing woman who was murdered by the Nazis when she was just thirty-eight years old.

> ✶ ✶ ✶

My father: Alexander Mozes

My father was a farmer. We owned just about all of the farmland surrounding the village. I can still remember how he set off early in the mornings on a horse and how we often brought him bread with butter. Somewhere out there, in the distance. We walked around while he worked next to us.

A stone's throw away from our house, just beyond the town boundary, we owned three apartments and a servant's house. Some of the workers and their families lived there; they worked in the fields and my father supervised them. He only got involved in the work himself when they needed additional help.

My father grew corn and wheat, as well as other crops. He often drove to the next major market squares in other towns.

I have to admit that I did not really like my father. I found him to be very extreme, particularly when it came to the topic of religion. He constantly complained that we were not raised religiously enough. My mother countered, "Come on, they are just children."

In retrospect, it seems to me that I was caught in an endless fight with my father. It was also due to the fact that I was the loudest of us girls. Whenever one of us needed something or was supposed to admit to something, my sister Edit sent me to the front. Compared to the others, Edit was a well-mannered girl; she wasn't even the littlest bit cheeky. I loved Edit a lot, and she probably had more influence on me than I realized at the time.

"You go first," she always told me. "You aren't afraid. You are also the only one who knows how you must talk to Dad. You can do it."

I felt so flattered by her that I did in fact go and engage my father in conversation. Usually it was about a request to go out somewhere or the desire not to say a prayer at lunchtime. Whatever it was, Edit always flattered me first, convincing me to talk to my father.

So I would bother my father. And I was beaten and punished for doing so, for having dared to ask him in Hungarian and not in Yiddish—which we could never speak, though. In turn, that meant that we had to sit quietly at the table during the whole mealtime.

One of my punishments was being locked in the dark pantry, where fruits and vegetables as well as preserves were stored. It was completely dark there. This is also where I developed my fear of mice. I could hear them jumping around and eating. I heard these mice pattering around everywhere. Later, in Auschwitz, I often remembered these times. I detested both the darkness and the mice.

However, I never seemed to learn my lesson. I was determined to forget my punishment and agreed to be the spokesperson each time someone was needed to talk to Dad. I continued to be taken in by their flattery, and my ego was inflated by the thought that I was the only one who could talk with him. Again the spokesperson—again the punishment. This fight between my father and me seemed as if it would never end.

He prayed every morning.

Now life on a farm means you are usually surrounded by animals. In our case, there was a huge number of cats and dogs. Most of them lived with us in the house. Before he began his prayers, my father often said to me, "Eva, could you throw all the dogs and cats out of the house so that they don't disturb my prayers?"

I obeyed.

However, cats and dogs are extremely clever. I was able to find them, but particularly on chilly days, I was unable to send them out of the house. If I recall correctly, we had two big beds in the kitchen. The dogs and cats hid as far as possible under the beds so that I was unable to get them out.

So it often came to pass that during my father's prayers, he would suddenly hear a "meow." Followed by a cat crawling out from under the bed. My father said nothing about it. At least not while he was praying. Afterward, he summoned me. "Eva?"

"Yes, Dad."

"Didn't I tell you to throw all the animals out of the house so that they wouldn't disturb me during my prayers?"

"Yes, Papa."

"Then why didn't you do it?"

"I did try to . . . ," I answered quietly.

"Then you didn't try hard enough. The cat disturbed my prayers."

"I'm sorry, Papa," I said cautiously.

"I am sorry too, Eva. Because you didn't do what I asked you to. Now I'll have to punish you."

I knew that there was no sense in protesting. So he spanked me.

I was the black sheep of the family—and that's no exaggeration. I despised my father for this procedure, and I thought it was completely inappropriate. My main thought in this time was "Just wait until I'm an adult. Then you will be small and I'll be big, and then I will hit you."

But it never came to that.

My sister Miriam, on the other hand, remembers him as a wonderful father. She recalls how he picked her up, put her on his lap, and told her stories. I cannot remember a single time that he picked me up and told me stories. I can only remember being put over his knee to be spanked.

Another problem between my father and me was that he had wanted a son. When I was younger, sometimes he would look at me and quietly say, "You should have been a son."

But it wasn't my fault that I was a girl. There was nothing I could do to change it. Either way, my father had no sons and, for some reason, he considered it my fault. It was almost as if my father thought everything about me was wrong.

He constantly gave me the feeling that I wasn't good enough. As if I had to constantly prove myself. On the other hand, I became more and more convinced that I was much better than the person he thought I was.

Perhaps that's what helped me survive.

Since my father's Jewish faith was so strong, our food was also blessed by him. One of the Jewish laws stipulates that you mustn't eat milk and meat together. This rule dates back to the times of Moses.

Back then, when Moses was in Egypt, this law was probably useful. I am sure that hygiene was not too closely observed. Lots of the meat on hand had probably been contaminated. In ancient times, maybe people even became ill because they had eaten milk and meat at the same time. Therefore, eating kosher offered the opportunity to avoid illnesses.

Another precept states that religious Jews may not drink milk for six hours after they have eaten meat. In addition, the meat must be prepared in a specific way, and no animal may be eaten which doesn't clean itself—for instance, pigs. Moreover, Jewish food must be prepared in kosher dishware. Dishes used for meat may not be used for dairy products, and by the same token, kosher dishware for dairy products may not come into contact with meat.

My father demanded that we follow these rules rigorously— just the way we were required to say our prayers. So when my mother dropped a fork on the ground, she had to boil the fork, and then my father said a special prayer over it because otherwise it would no longer be kosher.

Our meat also had to be slaughtered by a Jewish butcher who passed through a neighboring town once a week. We paid him a certain sum. He slaughtered the animal and bled it out with a ritual blessing. I even remember one summer when we hardly ate any meat for the sole reason that we could not store it in a ritualized way.

Alongside his morning prayers, my father was extremely strict when it came to keeping the Sabbath. It began on Friday evening at sunset. From this moment on, speaking Hungarian at the table was strictly forbidden; we were only allowed to speak Yiddish. However, we girls could hardly speak a word of Yiddish, so after sundown we didn't talk anymore. To me it was all pretty silly.

I asked myself each time, "Why didn't he ever teach us Yiddish?"

Today I sometimes wonder if my parents wanted to share a secret language that his children couldn't understand. This was definitely the case from 1943 onward, when the situation worsened. From then on they spoke Yiddish often, sometimes angrily.

Now the prayer regulation requires an assembly of ten people on the Sabbath or on holidays. And we were the only Jews in our village. The next town was three or four hours away, and the next town after that was an eight-hour drive. Therefore, the handful of Jews in the three surrounding towns gathered to form a recognized assembly. Each year, the assembly was held at a different house. The Jews made a pilgrimage to the selected house early in the morning and spent the day there in prayer. There were exact rules specifying when this had to begin.

I loved it when the participants met at another house because our father left the property early in the morning. Sometimes my mother also accompanied him, and a neighbor came over to babysit. Then we had a great time. We sisters locked the house and organized a picnic in the summer or winter garden. Then we ate chocolate cookies that our mother had prepared on our baking days and horsed around in high spirits. We played all the games that we were normally not even allowed to open and had tremendous fun. Although we were instructed to say our prayers, Father was not present to supervise us, so we didn't recite them.

I recall these days as beautiful, worry-free, peaceful times. We often played rummy with one another or read cheesy novels. We drank tons of milk, in which we dunked countless cookies, and all of that together was so fantastic that we could hardly wait for the next Sabbath.

When Father was finished saying his prayers, he drove home and interrogated us with a serious look as to whether we had said our prayers.

"Of course . . ."

In order to finish a whole book of prayers, we would have had to sacrifice half of Saturday. I didn't understand a word of what we murmured. Although I knew how to pronounce the words in Hebrew, I didn't know what they meant, even though I had recognized the letters ever since I was six years old. Nevertheless, the only word I could understand was the word for "God," since it was repeated so often.

Upon Father's return, if we were honest with him for some reason and told him that we hadn't finished our prayers, then he began to lead us in prayer in a loud, mechanical way until we had finished the prayer book. It was of the utmost importance to my father that the prayer book, which was meant for Saturday, was also finished every Saturday. There were also other special editions for other holidays.

I cannot remember whether my sisters really said their prayers in an intentional way. In any case, I did not. My only aim was to finish the whole thing as quickly as possible.

In Auschwitz it wasn't long before I realized, to my astonishment, how much this ability had benefitted me.

Maybe my descriptions of my father sound harsher than they should. That is not my intention—I loved him.

I believe my father would have been proud of me. He himself didn't have the chance to. This strong, proud man, firm in his convictions, died at the age of forty-four, in the prime of his life, in the gas chambers. In his honor, I named his grandson Alex.

* * *

Great suffering brings about great strength.

Nevertheless, I am still no fan of suffering. I survived Auschwitz, and with every new hurdle, I plead: *Please don't test me yet again.*

However, my wish was not heard and, instead, my life has been challenged over and over. I would have liked to have just one single week in my life in which I didn't have to solve various problems.

Nevertheless, in the combination of suffering and perseverance lies a secret passageway to happiness. This forces people to acknowledge that they have the inner strength and the mental tools to find a solution—along with the willingness to see themselves in a positive light.

The only other option is the path into drug and alcohol addiction.

But even when you are "stoned" and drunk, your own self still sits on your shoulder. That's why I always tell young people: Learn to like yourself. Be the best "you" that you can be. For a deep truth is—you can never be anyone else.

I would also like to weigh twenty pounds less, but with the medications I have to take, I am happy that I am still so good on my feet. I would have liked to be taller. A few more inches would have made my life easier on many occasions. But there is nothing I can do to change that. Those are the compromises you have to make.

When I was young, I was a good-looking girl. Always in action. Well, that has also changed with my age. Staying active becomes harder. I used to exercise with the kids; I did gymnastic stretches each morning.

Nevertheless, I have to like myself just the way I am.

Unfortunately I cannot shake the fact that I became a complete orphan when I was ten years old, and no one else will be able to wave a magic wand and make this rupture go away. But what I *can* change is my behavior and how I deal with this loss.

There are always two options: either I can sit in the corner and cry—which only gives me a headache and runny nose in the end—or I can consider matter-of-factly how I can survive in this world.

The conditions for survival are not subject to any testing standards, so I have to see how I can get by.

I realize that growing up is hard (even when you have loving parents at your side), and I am also aware that there are plenty of hardships on this planet, but if we want to raise our children to be self-sufficient, self-respecting individuals, then we cannot chew their porridge for them the rest of their lives. Certain hardships are part and parcel in life. On the other hand, if I give a child everything he desires, in the end I will raise a pampered, spoiled adult, whom no one will want to have anything to do with. Because our prince expects a life full of endowments and roasted doves.

We have to allow for difficulties in life in order to overcome them. And the first difficulty you successfully overcome remains anchored in your consciousness as one of the climaxes in your life. You will recall it again and again, and you will say, "Oh yes, I overcame these huge hurdles. And because I have successfully put them behind me, I can also tackle the next challenge."

This is why I always say to myself, *I have survived Auschwitz!* If I could manage to crawl over the filthy floor of the barracks for two weeks when I was deathly ill in order to survive, then I will settle any other problem in the world!

By the way, so far I have managed to catapult every other problem out of my life.

I still don't like these difficulties.

But I will never give up.

★ ★ ★

"What can I possibly do?"

Sometimes I receive letters from people expressing their helplessness when they hear about terrorism, war, and atrocities in the news.

For example, the people in Darfur, who have been threatened by genocide for over ten years, have almost been forgotten. And there is much that you can do.

One possibility would be to round up as many letters as humanly possible and send them to the Sudanese president, Omar al-Bashir or to the Chinese government. Or to the UN. I would like to appeal to all young people to get involved since children and young people are always the first among the victims in all genocides. Besides, children and young people have no voice to defend themselves, and they are not aware of what is happening around them.

I want to give them a voice. It's enough to send a letter without a complete address, without your last name. The simple act of raising your voice against this genocide is enough. And if you are afraid that such a letter could have uncomfortable consequences for you, then send your letter to the Holocaust Museum in Terre Haute, and I will send it for you.

It also does me good when I hear from young people who think like I do. In 2015, for example, another massacre shook the world community. A twenty-one-year-old, the son of a white family from the South, snuck into the Emanuel African Methodist Episcopal Church (AME) in Charleston, South Carolina, to shoot nine black people at random during a Bible study.

Sometime later, the parents of those killed publicly forgave the attacker. This act met with a lot of incomprehension. The public discussions culminated in the question, "How can relatives, how can we all endure such an unimaginable horror, such a form of viciousness?"

Unfortunately there is only one answer, and it's always the same answer: *We cannot change it.*

And in all of our misery, we have to call out to the perpetrators, "You will not destroy our hearts. And you will not destroy me by destroying my family members. For this reason, we will continue on this path. Every single one of us has decided to remain the person he or she was before. Instead of filling our hearts with hate, rage, and revenge, we are even reaching out to you with love and forgiveness."

This incident is one of the saddest events that I have heard about in a long time. You have to imagine—people are praying, and someone murders them while they are doing so because this person's thoughts are so full of hate and insanity.

So many extremists are filled with these muddled thoughts. How have they developed these extreme attitudes? I don't understand it. This young man could have had such a worry-free life, he could have given something positive to society, and instead he transformed it to a living nightmare.

⋆ ⋆ ⋆

There is a simple rule we should follow. In one word, it's equality. Or to put it another way, we should treat each other exactly the way we would like to be treated. It doesn't take any more than that!

We cannot control prejudices. Perhaps one day we could manage them the way banks are supposed to work, but otherwise, I think, it is primarily about teaching one another to like ourselves and value other people.

In my Holocaust Museum, we recently started a campaign borrowing Gandhi's words: "Be the change you want to see in the world!"

We also stretched a banner across the entire building with the slogan: "Let's wipe out all the hate and prejudice from the world—and let's begin with ourselves."

In most cases, a simple smile causes the other person to grin back. By the same token, when we give mean looks or use hate-filled gestures, then a similar repertoire will be used with us. (With one exception: if a person approaches us with a weapon, a smile will probably not change much.)

Ultimately, I have realized that it's all about becoming the person you would like to see in others. I have also decided to savor the beauty of the moment. No more is necessary in order to have a full life. And I can find this type of beauty in everything I am working on at the moment. Okay, maybe not in *everything*—but in each new day.

For example, very early in the morning, the birds are singing and the sun is just rising as I drink my tea on the porch, and one of the mail carriers delivers the newspaper. This moment can move me as much as a concert in Carnegie Hall. In winter, this overall composition is not possible in exactly this way, but in spring, summer, and even sometimes in fall, I enjoy this wonderful synchronicity between the sun, the birdsong, and the postal worker in the otherwise peaceful quiet.

In this mood, I even enjoy my gymnastic exercises later in the day. Because otherwise it's the worst thing that you can do to yourself. But when I can pull myself together to sweat for half an hour, then I notice my heart pumping and how thankful my body is and, at the same time, I know that I have put the worst part of the day behind me.

Exercise is also so important to me because I really like pizza. Fortunately, this has no negative consequences for me except for a few excess pounds. I also love sweets, but I have to hold off on these since I am borderline diabetic.

When I make an exception and eat sweets, I have to consume a lot of protein, or my blood sugar goes crazy. But all of that comes with old age. And this doesn't worry me as much as it perhaps should. I love pizza and chicken too much to care. And chocolate cake—when it comes to chocolate, period, I have a hard time saying no. And as I said, pizza is a particularly wonderful treat in winter when it's freezing outside.

However, food is no longer a reward for me. Indeed, it is harder for me to feel hunger pains and not be immediately catapulted into the past. And I don't just mean Auschwitz but also the later food shortages in Romania, where there was very little to eat and nothing of good quality.

Only ten years later, when I came to Israel, could I conscientiously control my eating habits for the first time without having to completely stuff myself. I was probably even overweight in Romania because I was constantly hungry; but then, when there was suddenly an opportunity to consume food, I devoured everything I could possibly eat.

That's why I disproportionately feel the growling in my stomach sometimes, and then I eat too much, because "starvation" is etched into my cerebrum. It's stronger than my actual desire to eat.

Otherwise there is only one ailment that can immediately transport me to the past, and that is when my toes are freezing. Then I could even tear down trees just to warm them up again.

So am I a peaceful Buddha type?

Sadly not.

When I say that I've forgiven the Nazis and emphasize the importance of forgiveness, it doesn't mean that nothing can fluster me. Sometimes even young people dressing up like idiots can drive me up a wall. Sometimes I still have to swallow when people throw things at my head—people with no decency who want to harm me.

However, what's decisive is that these high-pressure phases no longer pose a big problem for me. Precisely because I need to forgive, I can do so within a day or two. I am not longer willing to dwell on whatever has happened as a problem.

That's why I wouldn't even lose my temper if I saw Dr. Mengele on the street. I would approach him calmly, look him directly in the eyes, and ask him one crucial question, "What exactly did you inject into us back in Auschwitz?"

And then I would even add, "I forgive you. Not because you have earned it, but because I, along with every human being ever abused by you, deserve to be free."

Otherwise, Dr. Mengele plays no role in my everyday life. I lead an interesting life, and I could imagine many eighty-year-old people would like to whiz through the day the way I do. Even just the feeling of waking up early in the morning and having tons of interesting things to get started on. I talk with many young people, and they clearly enjoy what I have to say to them.

By no means do I sit around at home feeling sorry for myself. Instead, each day I try to cheer up people, to forgive them, and to encourage them never to give up—neither on themselves nor on their dreams, just as I never gave up, firmly convinced I would survive Auschwitz. I had no idea how I would make it, but it worked out.

Likewise, there are a huge number of people who don't know how they'll solve their problems each day. But if they give up, then nothing will happen at all!

Giving up is never an option. We have to try again and again until a solution finally emerges.

My certainty that this statement is true is perhaps one of the privileges of my advanced age.

I only focus on the solution because there is *always* a solution.

When I think back to the early 1980s, I was desperately looking for any expert who could pass on valuable information to the Mengele twins. I looked everywhere, again and again, to no avail, and I asked countless specialists over the years, but no one was dedicated to doing in-depth research on the murderous scientist Dr. Josef Mengele.

No German archive contained notes about his work or even the results of his gruesome genetic experiments. In the end, I had to admit one simple fact—when *I* am on the search for very specific information, then I cannot hope for someone *else* to come along by chance who is dedicated to it. I have to get up and look myself.

Of course, taking such a course is admittedly hard work, it means a lot of hassle, and yes, there is a risk that you'll be ridiculed and that you will merely bother people—but all your efforts can also lead to success.

Oh yes, you'll be able to gain a lot of friends when you are successful in something. A vast number of strangers will all suddenly want to be your friend.

It's only when you fail that no one is there to take the blame for you. They will all point the finger and make you alone responsible for failing.

Nevertheless.

That's why I also concentrate on medical ethics. I always tell doctors at my presentations that they are walking a thin line when they support clinical studies with human participants and forget that these studies have just one purpose: namely to help people, not to make a name for oneself in science. Otherwise, physicians risk sharing the same boat as Dr. Mengele. This man also thought he was onto the secret of the Aryan race and had long since forgotten that *humans* were freezing in front of him.

Today, when scientists can no longer exactly define whether their research is on a morally questionable path, then there is a relatively easy way to test one's conscience: just ask yourself whether you would do the tests on yourself, too. If the answer is *no*, then you are in the same boat as Mengele.

Sometimes people ask me if, in retrospect, I would change anything in my life. If I answered this question with even a qualified yes, I would be saying I want to give up control over life. But I like my life; I don't want to change anything. I like myself just the way I am. And I like what I do.

The only point that I'm clueless about at the moment is that despite my advanced age, I still give over 300 talks a year.

That is no longer manageable. But there must be a solution.

That's why I am considering the idea of no longer speaking for CANDLES myself everywhere, but asking like-minded people who support my life philosophy to act as ambassadors for me. Everywhere in the world.

Otherwise I have paid my dues; now let me harvest the fruits.

Never give up on yourself or your dreams, for everything good is possible in life. Judge people by their deeds and the core of their character.

Forgive your worst enemy and forgive every person who has hurt you—it will heal your soul and liberate you.

Apropos, I invite every reader to come celebrate the 100th anniversary of the liberation of Auschwitz with me—on January 27, 2045.

I will do my best to attend.

Will I see you there?